MEDIA ALERT!
200 Activities to Create Media-Savvy Kids

Sue Lockwood Summers

Hi Willow Research & Publishing
Castle Rock, Colorado
1997

CONTENTS

Review
Reflect
React

DEDICATION

This book is dedicated to Bob - my partner, husband, mentor, coach, editor, support system, and best friend!

ACKNOWLEDGMENTS

This book would not have been possible without the expertise of my husband who became my full-time editor, manager, and coach. I appreciate his partnership in this project and in all that I do. In addition, my deepest gratitude goes to Dan and Cheri Bidstrup at Word Graphics for the whimsical illustrations. Thanks to Shirley Sternola at Bo Peep Books for her valuable assistance and to the folks at Notre Dame Catholic School in Denver for their important validation of the activities.

PREFACE

A concerted effort to promote media literacy has been in existence for many years in countries such as Canada, Australia, England, New Zealand, and France. There have been a smattering of concerned educators and advocates in the United States, but until recently, media literacy has been almost nonexistent in U.S. schools. The goal of this book is to enable all adults - teachers, parents, scout leaders, counselors, Sunday School teachers, and youth leaders in general - to be part of the emerging media literacy movement.

In this book there are 50 media literacy "nuggets," each one representing a concept that is an integral component of media literacy. For each concept there is a specific goal the youngsters are to strive toward by completing age-appropriate learning activities. Activities are offered at four different age levels. Ongoing validation efforts indicate that each goal is attainable if the accompanying activities are completed. By using this book, any adult who is involved in teaching young people, whether in a traditional classroom or an out-of-school setting, can lead the children and youth through the learning exercises and thus help them become discerning and wise media consumers. In essence, these skills will enable youth to analyze, question, and evaluate all media messages and better understand the role of the mass media in their lives.

Community involvement to initiate a media literacy focus through Parent Teacher Associations, school districts, churches, service groups, and other organizations should be encouraged. These efforts should emphasize to mass media outlets, such as newspapers, cable companies, radio stations, and TV networks, that media literacy is not a threat, but is an emerging and exciting educational thrust that can produce positive results.

Media literacy is a dynamic field having the potential to revolutionize our culture. The pioneers in this movement have paved the way, and they should be applauded for their efforts. The hope is that the 200 activities in this book may serve as a springboard to integrate media literacy concepts into every home, school, and community.

INTRODUCTION

*There are two ways to slide easily through life; to believe everything or
to doubt everything. Both ways save us from thinking.*

Alfred Korzybski

In a time when the mass media have so saturated our society that our children are literally immersed in messages from the day of their birth, it is urgent that we begin to understand the mass media and their impact. Stewart Hoover, a communications professor at the University of Colorado, says that asking someone to analyze our culture is like asking a goldfish to analyze the water. We are so totally immersed that it is virtually impossible to step back and take notice of what is happening. One doesn't need to be a sociologist or scholar to observe that the mixed messages and varied values being emitted through the media have influenced us all. Even for those who do not own a television (and that is only about 1% of the total population), it is evident that the TV alone has a shaping influence on everything around us. Add to that the multitude of other electronic media and the incessant bombardment of print media and we may indeed face the consequences of overload. Merely wringing our hands or using the media as convenient scapegoats will not lessen their impact. Fortunately, there is now something constructive that we can do; we can take a pro-active role and become involved in media literacy training for all young people, allowing them to become knowledgeable and discerning citizens. Thus, this book. It's contents include 200 specific activities aimed at the entire range from preschool children through high school youth. The book is written to be used - not just read.

The media surround each of us every day with a variety of information and entertainment options. To keep children, teenagers, and even adults from being manipulated by the highly motivated and skillful media makers, adult leaders must teach them to be media literate - thus developing a media-savvy generation. Successful completion of the learning activities in this book will enable participants to be critical thinkers about the content and format of the messages, their marketing and distribution, and their significant impacts.

Where do children get their values? Children and teenagers internalize values from adults they respect. In many cases these adults are parents, but upon careful reflection of who were the strongest influences in our early lives, we are likely to discover there were others - perhaps a 4th grade teacher, a neighbor, or a Sunday School teacher. It is possible that a grandparent, a counselor, or a youth leader had a lasting effect; whoever it was, it was someone we respected. The same is true for today's younger generation.

In many homes, negative messages from popular music, video games, movies, and TV programs can seem alluring and powerful to a child starving for meaning in his world. Dr. Paul King, author of *Sex, Drugs, and Rock 'n Roll,* writing about the impact of popular music, stated:

"Glorification of negative power is the common thread in heavy metal, hard core, and some rap music. The marketing and commercialization seems to say that what's bad is good, what's evil is great, and what treats women as dirt is macho and wonderful. It has a powerful attraction for young people who feel inadequate, insecure, and helpless. In a pro-social situation, positive power comes from work, school, sports, church, and other service activities. Young people can feel adequate and powerful in a negative way, however, by doing drugs and getting into the culture of negative music. Adolescents reach this stage not merely by listening to the music, but by adopting it as a philosophy of life. The adolescent feels very powerful in being antisocial."

(Adolescent Counselor, Oct./Nov. 1989)

In contrast, the adult who is involved in positive activities with a child or teenager can help sort through the daily positive, negative, and neutral messages that flow from the mass media. Appropriate standards for attitudes, beliefs, and behavior come from adults who have developed a strong rapport with the young person.

This chapter introduces the reader to the book through the following sections: Rationale, Format, Process, and Additional Resources. It provides the necessary foundation for concerned adults involved in the lives of young children and teenagers to jump in and get started in the media literacy process.

RATIONALE:

Media literacy is defined as the ability to access, analyze, evaluate, and communicate information in a variety of formats, both print and non-print. In essence, media literacy refers to the skills and knowledge needed to question, analyze, interpret, and evaluate those messages that are created and disseminated by the mass media. Print media include newspapers, magazines, books, advertising fliers and billboards, clothing, signs, and other static messages. Non-print media include television, radio, movies, cassette tapes and CDs, videotapes, the Internet, and other electronic modes of communication.

Training in media literacy requires hands-on activities and specific opportunities for learners to acquire the requisite knowledge and skills involved in critical thinking. This can certainly happen within the classroom setting or at home, but should also occur at a Boy Scout or Girl Scout troop meeting, a Sunday School class, a church youth group, a home school, a preschool, a residential youth facility, or any other location where adults are willing to help young people develop a foundation for critical thinking. In the supersaturated schedule of the formal school environment, teaching media literacy requires an integrated approach that incorporates it into curricula at all levels from preschool through high school. However, to restrict this training to just the school setting limits its effectiveness. For example, preschool children need media literacy training because they watch so much TV. In other words, this learning process must take place everywhere - in the home, school, church, and community - to ensure that the current generation is not easily manipulated by the myriad techniques and motivations of the media.

Although media literacy is sometimes seen primarily in the context of creating wiser consumers, the necessity to encourage deeper thought in regards to politics, ethics, the judicial system, corporate responsibilities, and societal norms must certainly be addressed. Media literacy training encourages positive participation in the culture.

By merging media literacy into the school, home, church, and community, and even into media presentations themselves, an awareness campaign is likely to result. Wide-spread critical thinking about the messages from the mass media may lead to possible solutions for many of our present cultural concerns. Some of these are complex problems that need to be dealt with directly: drug addiction, crime, teen pregnancy, promiscuous sex, materialism, violence, racism, eating disorders, tobacco and alcohol consumption by teens and younger children, sexual and physical abuse, profanity, voter apathy, and pornography. These must be addressed not with insular programs but through comprehensive culture-based efforts that are sufficiently broad in scope to reach all entities of the community. In this way, media literacy can be the catalyst for sweeping and lasting reform.

Media literacy training should begin with preschool children, with the goal of introducing specific concepts and fostering interactive thinking about various media-related topics. As the children continue this critical thinking process through their elementary school, middle school, and high school years, ongoing exposure to media literacy activities will challenge them to think critically about the many diverse aspects of the mass media.

Just as doing only twenty push-ups on one day will not automatically create a stronger and healthier body, completing only one media literacy activity cannot develop a competent critical thinker. It is the combination of stimulating activities and the continued encouragement by adults that can result in wiser and more analytical young people. To begin the process at the preschool level and continue it throughout the child's developmental years establishes a strong foundation for lifelong critical thinking. By beginning as soon as the media become part of their daily lives, children can be expected to develop the skills necessary to interpret and evaluate those mediated messages as they experience them.

There seem to be two camps in the media literacy movement. The first is protectionist in nature, and is comprised of those who would restrict the media's messages and limit the involvement their children have with the negative and less desirable messages from the media. The other camp, the free speech advocates, believe that we need only arm our youth with the skills and knowledge they must have to de-construct and evaluate all messages they encounter. These two groups have one thing in common: they want children and teenagers to embrace the positive messages and become pro-active in their selection process, rather than be manipulated by media-makers to devolve to the culture's least common denominator. This is one instance in which it is not necessary to join the same camp, as long as the motivation is the welfare of young people in the development of critical thinking skills.

It is not the goal of media literacy training to create cynics. As can be seen in the figure below, there is literally a continuum of thinkers, with sponges on one end and cynics on the other.

CRITICAL THINKING CONTINUUM

Sponges - - - - - - - - - Healthy Skeptics - - - - - - - - Cynics

Sponges absorb everything they see, hear, or read and assume it is all true. Cynics dismiss everything they see, hear, or read and assume it is all incorrect or possibly even a plot with some conspiracy against them. The truly media literate citizen must be a healthy skeptic - with skills to judge the reliability of the sources of the information, to verify the validity of the facts, and finally to reflect on the meaning and impact on personal life. However, these skills are not innate; they must be learned and practiced over a period of time.

There is truly a love-hate relationship with the media - we love 'em and we hate 'em. Many people are quick to bash the mass media and imply that society's ills are their fault. It is standard practice to speak with disdain about television, Hollywood, the news industry, and advertising. However, as a culture, we continue to spend an increasing amount of time involved in media experiences. Positive effects of the mass media are well documented, particularly in the areas of education, politics, health and safety, and current events. The mass media are responsible for social change, the democratic process, knowledge of world events, and consumer education. In reality, few people would be willing to live without a free press. Journalists keep politicians on their toes, corporations in check, and problems in the spotlight. The print and electronic media can directly benefit society with information, warnings, and exposés. It is clear that discernment and selection become necessary skills in an age of mixed messages.

As the mass media continue to become the most influential institution in our society, it is imperative that citizens develop the capacity to review, reflect, and react to all media messages on a personal basis. As delineated below, these three steps, the 3 Rs, attempt to restate the critical thinking process as it applies to the messages from the mass media.

REVIEW Review the actual content of the presentation. After viewing a sitcom, for instance, take time to think about the story, its message, the characters, the setting, the dialog, etc. Some appropriate questions are:
- How realistic was it?
- Was there a moral?
- Was some of the language offensive?
- Was it accurate?
- Was it entertaining?
- How timely was the message?

REFLECT Reflect on both the content and the format of the message. Writing in a journal can encourage this aspect of critical thinking. Take time to actively consider what the message was. Personal beliefs, ideas, and opinions are used to evaluate all incoming messages. After reading a magazine ad, for example, consider:
- Do I agree or disagree with the ad's statements?
- What, if any, difference will it make in my life?
- How do I feel about the content and the format?
- Who was the intended audience? Was it directed at me?
- Did the people or characters in the ad represent me, my family, or my friends?
- Did it encourage or offend me?
- Who sponsored this message and why?
- Is this information reliable?
- Does it present a biased viewpoint?

REACT React to the message. Take a stand or decide on an action. After watching a newscast, for instance, your opinion may be changed regarding a social issue. Perhaps this will cause you to vote - in favor of a local candidate or against a new ordinance. Reaction to a message might merely reaffirm an existing idea or opinion. After reading an editorial, for instance, you may feel more convinced than ever about your opposition to a new shopping mall in your area. Reacting may result in a personal decision about time, money, behavior, or attitudes. Some considerations might be:
- What can I do to support this issue?
- What can I do to oppose this project?
- Should I buy that product?

These 3 Rs make up the foundation for the media literacy process throughout this book. First you review exactly what you heard, read, or saw. Next you reflect on the content, format, and meaning for you personally. Then you react to the message. Each of the pages in this book reinforces this critical thinking process. Some activities directly involve one of these steps. In other cases the 3 Rs are integrated into discussions or assignments. In all, critical thinking about the messages of the media is the goal.

FORMAT:

The style and presentation of information in this book is different than most. This is a collection of easy-to-use and effective activities and discussion starters for four age groups: preschool, elementary school, middle school, and high school. If, for instance, the reader is a third grade teacher, there are 50 different media literacy exercises that are specifically geared to a class of elementary aged children. If, on the other hand, the reader is a parent or youth leader with children of various ages, there are a variety of age-appropriate activities aimed at each of the groups to help develop critical thinking skills. A youth pastor, for example, might use the activities written for high school participants as a means of stimulating the teenagers in the youth group to learn to evaluate media messages.

This collection of 200 graded activities is meant to jump-start the thinking process by serving as an introduction to important media literacy concepts. Each of the 50 activity pages contains, in this order, the following segments:

- the media literacy skill (the goal)
- a statistic or quotation (rationale/motivation)
- the concept (summary of background information, vocabulary, and purpose)
- preschool-1st grade activities
- elementary school activities
- middle school activities
- high school activities
- supplemental resources (where appropriate)

This book contains 50 media literacy concepts - each one a nugget that serves as the background for the activities on that page. Because media literacy is an umbrella term that refers to the critical thinking about the messages of the mass media, breaking it into distinct, easily-digestible morsels results in a more manageable critical thinking diet. Even a 4-year-old can discuss his media world and analyze cartoons, cereal boxes, and picture book characters. Through age-appropriate activities all children are provided opportunities to review, reflect, and react - thereby becoming critical thinkers.

Each learning activity listed on the 50 pages serves as a basic starting point and requires a minimum of materials and resources. Each activity could be further developed into a series of lessons or a formal media literacy unit, but in its present form serves as an opportunity to start training children and teenagers to be media savvy.

The preschool-through-1st grade activities are meant for non-readers and do not assume any level of reading ability. Preschool, kindergarten, and 1st grade children are capable of discussing and digesting a multitude of new concepts. Each of these activities is geared to the 4-, 5-, and 6-year-old child's level. This activity might involve one child in the home, a small group at a preschool or church, or an entire class of children in a school. The goal of this activity is to introduce an idea and encourage discussion of a construct that enables the child to have the requisite foundation for further investigation and contemplation in later childhood. To those who would say this is too early to begin the media literacy process, consider that the average child has already seen 5,000 hours of television before entry into 1st grade; it is certainly not too early to begin introducing the skills and knowledge needed to analyze and evaluate mass media messages.

Continuing the media literacy process in elementary school allows children to further investigate TV, advertising, movies, computerized information, print materials, and music messages. By this age, children are well-versed in popular culture themes. They are likely to find, for example, that the current Disney movie has infiltrated every aspect of their world, from McDonald's Happy Meal toys to clothing and even to theme music aired on the radio or over department stores' PA systems. Elementary-age children can learn to compare and contrast, investigate, examine, and evaluate the messages and the media's distribution tactics. Encouraging elementary-age children to analyze the entertainment and advertising world helps to ensure that they will be less susceptible to enticing marketing ploys.

Middle school-age adolescents, as a rule, have attached themselves wholeheartedly to their Nintendo, MTV, and "Beverly Hills 90210" world. It is imperative that they distance themselves intellectually and evaluate these messages more objectively before they are trapped in an entertainment lifestyle. This age group can be the hardest to guide into critical thinking since, due to peer pressure, they often want to buy into the popular culture's themes. Journal writing is introduced as a learning activity at this developmental level to cause the participants to reflect on selected topics and new information so they can formulate their own thoughts and analysis. Journal writing is personal and allows the participants to truly be individuals and escape the reactions of their peers. All students at the junior and senior high level should be encouraged to keep journals.

High school teenagers make value judgments and decisions about the mass media that may later affect their lifestyles. Adults they emulate, what messages they believe, and the information sources they trust may set in place permanent patterns. It is imperative that high school youth be given specific opportunities and encouragement to explore their mediated world, to create media messages, and to assess the range of the mass media's impact on their culture. Information and entertainment sources vie for their time, money, and allegiance. By being introduced to basic media literacy concepts, teenagers will have the foundation for lifelong critical thinking about the role of the media in their culture.

A common assumption in our society is that learning happens only in a formal school setting. It's an established fact that children and teenagers learn wherever there is a relevant reason for assimilating new meaningful information. What could be more relevant than learning about the media world in which they are immersed! A Sunday School teacher, a scout leader, a counselor, or a parent, for instance, is sure to have opportunities to lead discussions, create learning opportunities, and guide the examination of the world of television, news, advertising, movies, print, and music. In reality, teachers often avoid these topics. It will take a combination of adults in the school, home, church, and community to help young people become discerning critical thinkers.

Following the 50 activity pages, there is a glossary (mini-dictionary) of media-related terms that are mentioned in this book. It provides the opportunity to define terms that are used on some of the 50 activity pages. In addition, it can serve as a vocabulary list for youth to become more adept at mass media concepts.

Because this book serves as a starting place for those adults interested in creating media-savvy children, the 200 activities are designed to whet the appetites of youngsters who may want to further investigate these topics. The Additional Resources section will allow the reader to access other media literacy instructional materials and organizations that provide instructional materials, conferences, newsletters, and workshops.

THE PROCESS:

Children and teenagers are looking for direction and approval. They will find it in caring adults who take time to discuss, listen, and encourage interaction and personal reflection. Despite the constant bombardment of mixed messages from print and electronic media, one caring adult can still make a difference in the life of a child.

The process to be applied in these learning activities is quite straightforward. After selecting one of the 50 specific skills, read the accompanying concept. Keep in mind the concept is the basis for the entire scope of activities. All the activities developed for this book meet accepted criteria for effective learning. They involve the participants in authentic tasks using meaningful materials - actual samples from the mass media. Group members are required to review, reflect, react, deconstruct, analyze, evaluate, and use higher-level thinking. Only realistic activities are used, so the participants get practice in the skills they are to develop. Because the facilitator is encouraging the participants to be actively engaged in the media literacy process, children and youth are highly motivated to participate in discussions and to develop and conduct the prescribed surveys and interviews. These activities get them involved with professionals and other adults who have expertise in areas being studied. Such projects also provide experience in personal interactions and in analyzing results of the surveys and interviews. Furthermore, the increased exposure to the interworkings of the media and the making of media products may be an encouragement for some participants to seek careers in media-related fields.

It must be emphasized that the 50 concepts are not linear; that is, the order in which the facilitator selects them is an individual matter. The order of selection should be predicated upon the readiness of the learners. Each learner will approach the activities with a unique readiness based on personal knowledge, experiences, and interests. In addition, the learners can make some movement along the critical thinking continuum without accomplishing all the prescribed activities. However, each completed activity will strengthen their foundation and enhance the thinking of the children or teenagers. Because media literacy is an umbrella term for critical thinking about the messages of the mass media, it is essential that the skills addressed in these learning activities be internalized if participants are to be considered media-savvy.

A media-savvy generation will expect the mass media to present accurate information, balanced representations, and positive role models.

> One's mind, once stretched by a new idea, never regains its
> original dimensions.
>
> Oliver Wendall Holmes

1. REVIEW

...Swift as is the delivery of the radio bulletin, graphic as is television's eyewitness picture, the task of adding meaning and clarity remains urgent. People cannot and need not absorb meaning at the speed of light.

Erwin Canham

CONCEPT:

The first step in critical thinking is to review what is read, seen, or heard. The fast-paced media bombardment from television and other mass media does not provide time to review. For example, one TV commercial follows another, and a new program segment starts immediately after the commercials. The processing of text, images, and audio messages from the electronic and print media is an essential part of being a critical thinker in a media-saturated society.

ACTIVITIES:

Preschool - 1st Grade

Read a picture book to the children displaying all of the illustrations. After finishing the book, ask questions about the content, sequence, characters, plot, and illustrations. Discuss specific details of the illustrations. Review the story, especially the characters, sequence, consequences, and special moments.

Elementary School

Have/help the children read a news article from an age-appropriate publication. Make a composite list of all information contained in the story. Discuss the reasons the event occurred, where it happened, who was involved, and whether it could happen again.

Middle School

Have the group members watch videotaped TV commercials they probably have not seen before, such as old commercials or some from the middle of the night. After showing 10-12, give them a quiz on specific inconsequential details concerning the products or companies. Discuss why viewers have trouble remembering all the information. Is it possible to absorb all of the specific details in such a fast presentation? Why is it essential to review what is seen, heard, or read?

High School

Have participants compare and contrast a news story from a TV news report with the same news story in print. Are the details the same? What are the differences? Are the differences significant? How could the reporting of a news item be so different? Review other news stories to compare their facts. Discuss the findings.

REVIEW
REFLECT
REACT

2. REFLECT

To read without reflecting is like eating without digesting.
Edmund Burke

CONCEPT:

Reflecting is the second step in the critical thinking process. Reflecting on a media message means comparing it to our own value system, the values of our family, our church, and our community. Reflecting asks that we determine who is trying to affect our behavior, why, and whether to allow our own thinking to be influenced by the message.

ACTIVITIES:

Preschool - 1st Grade

Allow children to make their own choices about as many different aspects of their days as possible. Talk about individual likes and dislikes. Some like one color paint; some like another. Discuss those times where there are no choices and rules must be followed, such as specific rules regarding health, safety, social interactions, etc. Help children distinguish between areas of choice and areas of obedience.

Elementary

Read and discuss a picture book that invokes personal responses and interpretations. Some suggestions of books that might stimulate reflection are:
- *When the New Baby Comes, I'm Moving Out* by Martha Alexander
- *Alexander and the Terrible, Horrible, No Good, Very Bad Day* by Judith Viorst
- *The Piggybook* by Anthony Browne

Middle School

Read aloud a magazine article (e.g. from the *Reader's Digest*) about a topic or idea that is new to the group. Initiate an open-ended discussion about the ramifications of the information, encouraging thoughtful comments. Ask the group members to listen to each other and communicate their own ideas. Have them reflect on the information in their journal entries.

High School

Have participants choose an important social issue. Over the course of a few weeks have them read and collect news items from the print media on their topics. Assign daily journal entries concerning thoughts/observations/reflections about these news stories. Allow each participant to lead a group discussion, sharing new information, thoughts, and observations.

3. REACT

*A good education can't make leaders out of all of us, but it can
teach us which leaders to follow.*

Unknown

CONCEPT:

Critical thinking often results in a change - a change in attitude, behavior, or life direction. Messages from the mass media can trigger personal reactions and even social reform. For example, a reaction to tonight's news might lead to involvement in a political campaign. A reaction to the new movie about an important social issue might lead to the library for further investigation. The more often people react to mass media messages, the less likely they are to be manipulated by them.

ACTIVITIES:

Preschool - 1st Grade

Read aloud a picture book that deals with a problem such as:
- *Farewell to Shady Glade* by Bill Peet
- *The Butter Battle Book* by Dr. Seuss
- *The Great Kapok Tree* by Lynne Cherry

Encourage the children to brainstorm solutions to the problem.

Elementary School

Watch a videotape that focuses on a social issue, such as the environment or a community problem. Discuss concerns. Allow the children time to express their ideas about what could be done. Plan a group project to have children do something about a specific problem themselves. Analyze the impact of their actions over time.

Middle School

Have group members read newspaper editorials and letters to the editor about a specific issue and discuss possible choices for action. Assign a written essay or oral argument about possible remedies. Carry out an action project with them and analyze the impact of their work over time.

High School

Invite a panel of knowledgeable adults to discuss a current problem, such as violence on TV. Have participants ask questions about possible solutions. Have them create a survey to poll family members or other adults about their ideas for solutions to the problem and tally the data. Allow discussion time to react to both the problem and the suggested solutions. As a group, select one significant action they can take. Complete it, and analyze the results over a period of time. Discuss whether they have accomplished the results they had hoped for.

*Review
Reflect
React*

4. IDENTIFY "DESCRIBING" WORDS

Snap! Crackle! Pop!
Kellogg's registered trademark for Rice Krispies Cereal

CONCEPT:

Words are powerful tools that can be used to inspire, encourage, motivate, or sway. In advertising and news reporting, for instance, the selection of the words is very important. Each word is deliberately chosen to influence or capture attention. In the case of a headline, puns may imply humor or a light-hearted story. The selection of an emotional word, though, can evoke anger, compassion, or sympathy. Children and teenagers must be made aware that words are often chosen to elicit specific reactions.

ACTIVITIES:

Preschool - 1st Grade

Read aloud a story that contains lots of describing words. Discuss those words, as well as other words that describe things. Have the group think of words that are opposites, such as happy and sad, and then replace some words with their opposites during the second reading of the story. How does that change the meaning and the children's reactions?

Elementary School

Have children select and look at magazine ads, cut out all describing words, and place them on a posterboard or bulletin board. Conduct a discussion of the words' impact on their attitudes, opinions, choices, etc. Have them choose their favorite words and identify those that elicit emotional reactions.

Middle School

Have small groups of participants select a news story or editorial from the newspaper and circle or list all of the adjectives in the article. Then have the group create a continuum of adjectives, with positive words at one end and negative words at the other. Have each group reread the selected article and replace each adjective with a word from the opposite end of the continuum. Rewrite the article with the new adjectives and discuss the new version. Did the replaced words alter either the facts or their perceptions?

High School

Have the teenagers watch for emotional or biased words being used in TV news reports or in newspapers or news magazines. Discuss their impact. Have the group watch or read political campaign ads, focusing on the emotionally-charged words. Ask them to create an ad for a fictitious product and rewrite the text a number of times, each time using different describing words. Share the ads. In each instance, analyze changes in the ad's impact.

5. CLASSIFY AS REAL OR MAKE-BELIEVE

*When viewers become seduced by TV's aura of authenticity, the
potential exists for distorted reality to become society's reality.*
Howard Rosenberg, TV critic, *L. A. Times*

CONCEPT:

According to the famous psychologist, Jean Piaget, children cannot clearly distinguish between what is real and what is fantasy until approximately seven or eight years of age. Although children entering the first grade have already seen an average of 5000 hours of TV, most of them still need help understanding what is real and what is make-believe. Even teenagers and adults may struggle with this cognitive process amidst the technology of computer-enhanced photography and animation that is so real it's believable. The dinosaurs in the movie, "Jurassic Park," or the "re-creation" of deceased presidents in "Forrest Gump" keep audiences guessing. On television, reality-based dramas such as "Rescue 911," "Unsolved Mysteries," and "America's Most Wanted" interweave real scenes with re-enacted ones. The line between reality and fantasy is intentionally blurred.

ACTIVITIES:

Preschool - 1st Grade

Show a videotaped TV commercial to the children. Discuss whether the characters are real people, animated drawings, or a combination of both. Were they actors, hired to speak their lines and perform, or were they people honestly discussing a service or product? When people dress in costumes, are they "real?" Is Barney "real?" Have the children think of examples of make-believe characters.

Elementary School

Have the children read an article in a newspaper. Analyze the event. Was it real or staged? Was this story factual? Was anyone paid to be involved? How do you know whether it is accurate? Is everything you read "real?"

Middle School

Watch a TV "reality drama" (a program based on real-life situations that contains dramatizations, such as "Rescue 911"). Are the people real? Is any portion of this program a dramatization? Does the use of actors change the program's impact? Does paying people to represent real events cause the audience to be confused about reality and make-believe? Discuss whether a reality drama is fact or fiction.

High School

Have each participant select and read three elementary-level biographies written about the same person. Compare and contrast the facts stated in the books. Were there any discrepancies? Discuss whether conversations or situations are ever "made up" in a biography. How are biographies different from novels? Have each person write an autobiography.

6. DISCRIMINATE BETWEEN FACT AND OPINION

Don't judge me by what you've heard about me, judge me by what I do.

Rupert Murdoch, media owner

CONCEPT:

Facts are real and provable information. Opinions, on the other hand, are the thoughts, feelings, or personal attitudes of individuals. To understand any message, it is important to distinguish between fact and opinion. Facts can be found in various print and electronic media through sources such as newspapers, books, the Internet, television, and radio. Opinions are usually found in television and radio commentaries or on the editorial or "op-ed" pages of newspapers. Opinions are sometimes intentionally integrated into otherwise factual portions of a news program or article, resulting in biased or unfair reporting. A strategy that embodies both facts and opinions is the debate.

ACTIVITIES:

Preschool - 1st Grade

Have children discuss the difference between a fact and an opinion and give examples of both. Show a taped 30-second commercial from children's TV programming (kidvid). Watch for facts and opinions and then discuss both categories. Then have them view additional TV ads on other occasions, each time finding and discussing the facts and opinions.

Elementary School

Have everyone in the group read the same news story or column in a news publication, circling all the facts and underlining the opinions in the piece. Discuss the reasons for their selections. Give the same article to a person outside the group to do the same thing. Discuss why there could be differences in the labeling of fact and opinion. Repeat the activity with other news articles.

Middle School

Have members study editorials and letters to the editor in the newspaper and have each choose a topic that generates strong feelings. Have each member write a letter that contains specific facts and personal opinions. Send letters to the editor of the school newspaper, a local newspaper, or post them on an Internet home page.

High School

Stage a debate. Participants are to decide on the topic or social issue to be debated and delineate the two sides of the debate. They must spend adequate time researching facts to support their opinions. During the debate have each team and members of the audience keep scorecards that note facts and opinions stated. After the debate, compare the results, listing facts and opinions that were presented by each side. Are there discrepancies? Why? Can the same fact be used to support different opinions? Discuss the ramifications of this idea.

7. RECOGNIZE PRODUCT PLACEMENT

As a result of the placement in 'The Firm' [movie], Red Stripe sales have increased 53% from a comparative period last year.
Marco Moretti, Brand Manager, Red Stripe Beer,
Dateline, 1994

CONCEPT:

Product placement refers to the intentional and readily-identifiable appearance of brand name products in movies, TV shows, and video games. Although they are used in a manner that appears to be haphazard and innocuous, these commercial items are meant to persuade viewers that these are the norm, and should be considered "standard equipment." We are more vulnerable, and therefore influenced by such brand names, because we are not anticipating a commercial message. The average viewer might claim to ignore or be resistant to such ploys; however, if that were true, companies would not be spending money to place their products in the eyes of the masses.

ACTIVITIES:

Preschool - 1st Grade

Have the children, as a group, watch the "Reese's Pieces" segment of the movie, "ET." Discuss the use of the candy. Have the children tell whether they have ever tasted Reese's Pieces. Did the movie make them want to taste this candy? Why?

Elementary School

Have children discuss the idea of product placement. Have them make a composite list of hidden ads they have seen in movies, in video games, and on TV. Discuss the purpose of these hidden ads. Should these ads be allowed? Why? Have each child draw a picture with different brand name products displayed in the scene. Share the pictures and discuss the products.

Middle School

Discuss product placement. Discuss movies and other entertainment media where they have seen brand name product placements. Have participants keep a running log of the media they view during a two-week period, listing the programs or movie titles and all of the recognizable products. Discuss the purpose and effects of product placement.

High School

Discuss the concept of product placement. Have participants keep track over a two-week period of all hidden ads they see in movies, TV shows, and video games. Have them express their opinions about product placement by writing to the companies. Discuss "political placement" - carefully placed conscience-raising messages that promote social causes. Have participants do research to determine ownership of the various movie and TV studios, and trace other companies and products they own. Can such ownership affect product placement in TV programs and movies? Have them write a journal entry on this topic.

RESOURCES:

"Buy Me That, Too" video, segment on product placement. (See Additional Resources section.)

REVIEW
REFLECT
REACT

8. IDENTIFY PRODUCT CROSS-OVERS

*...As many as 300 million Dole banana clusters will carry
stickers for the new feature 'Muppet Treasure Island.'*

KidScreen, February, 1996

CONCEPT:

When two otherwise unrelated companies join together to market items that benefit both businesses, the process is called "cross-merchandising" or "product cross-over." One obvious example is the marketing of free toys with kids' meals at fast-food restaurants. It is common practice for these restaurants to offer toys that are related to newly released movies, even though the restaurants do not directly benefit from the box office revenues. It is important to recognize that companies work together to increase both companies' profits.

ACTIVITIES:

Preschool - 1st Grade

Discuss the toys that come with kids' meals at fast food restaurants. Have the children ever received kids' meal toys that were related to a new movie? Name some. Ask why they think the movie toys are included with the meals. Do these toys make children more eager to see the movie? In addition, does seeing the movie make them more anxious to get the free toys? Why?

Elementary School

Take a survey to see how many children have seen movie-related toys with kids' meals at fast food restaurants. Discuss why the toys are in the meals. Have they ever seen board games or video games related to new movies? Why are McKids clothes sold at Walmart but not at McDonald's restaurants? Introduce and discuss the concept of product cross-overs.

Middle School

Examine the group for clothing items (hats, T-shirts, shoes, etc.) that advertise sports teams or popular products. Discuss teen willingness to advertise some name brands but not others. Why do some companies promote other companies' merchandise? Introduce and discuss the concept of product cross-overs. Invite a local sports coach to talk about equipment and uniform sponsorships and the benefits to both parties. Encourage questions and discuss the speaker's responses.

High School

Have group members discuss the product cross-over concept. Then have them watch for product cross-overs during the next week and analyze their findings. Have small groups develop simulated companies creating products that would appeal to children or teenagers. Have each group brainstorm ways for other groups' companies to market and merchandise their products. Discuss these ideas.

9. ANALYZE VIOLENT MESSAGES IN ENTERTAINMENT

The average child will see 8,000 murders on TV by the time he finishes elementary school.

"Facts About Television," TV-Free America

CONCEPT:

Webster's New Collegiate Dictionary defines violence as "the exertion of physical force so as to injure or abuse." Much of today's entertainment is delivered via books, movies, television programs, video games, music lyrics, and computer games that increasingly contain violent messages and images. When violence occurs as entertainment, it rarely seems as real or terrifying as it is in real life. Violence in entertainment may then desensitize the audience to its insidious effects. Numerous scientific studies have indicated that violence in the entertainment media appears to increase aggressive behavior.

ACTIVITIES:

Preschool - 1st Grade

Have children define violence in their own words and then list examples of violence. Watch a videotaped TV cartoon that includes violence. Why is there violence in cartoons? Is real-life violence funny and harmless? Discuss this topic whenever there are new cartoons, movies, or ads that seem violent.

Elementary School

Have children define violence and list examples of it. Have them take the list home and as they watch TV over the next week, make a check mark next to each act of violence as they see it. Discuss in the group what they saw and whether there were any consequences of the violence. How realistic was the televised violence? Discuss violence in popular fiction books. Discuss real-life consequences of violence.

Middle School

Define violence, including verbal violence (profanity). Have participants discuss movies and TV shows they have seen that contained violence. Why is there violence in entertainment? Discuss what long-term effects might result from "visual violence." Have them research studies on violence in the media and report their findings to the group. Ask prominent people in the community or in the media industry to attend this reporting session and to share their reactions.

High School

Have participants select a children's program or cartoon (kidvid), such as "X-Men" or "Mighty Morphin' Power Rangers," that is known to contain violence. As a group, brainstorm and create an extensive checklist of possible violent actions. Watch the selected children's TV program and use the checklist to tally all violent actions. Have them react to the show's violence by writing or e-mailing a message directly to the creators or sponsors of the program. Have them research whether sponsors are aware in advance of the content of their programs. Discuss the findings.

THE RIALTO THE RIALTO
Review   Review
Reflect React Reflect React

10. ANALYZE VIOLENCE IN THE NEWS

Taken together as the 'Mayhem Index' of newscasts, stories about crime, disaster and war average 42% of the news on all 100 stations. These topics have in common a focus on violent events that can purvey fear and alienation to the audience. These are the most toxic life-threatening emotions.
"Pavlov's TV Dogs," Rocky Mountain Media Watch

CONCEPT:

The news industry is economically driven and must therefore be concerned with ratings and sales revenue. Sensational stories and graphic images may increase TV newscast viewership and newspaper or news magazine sales. Both the print and electronic news deliver stories that are violent. Violence in the news is real, but we tend to become immune to it much as we have to the entertainment violence. In other words. it is possible for us to become desensitized to the suffering of others.

ACTIVITIES:

Preschool - 1st Grade

Ask children to define "violence" and give some examples of violent actions. Have they ever seen violent scenes on TV or in the movies? Does violence ever happen in real life? Discuss real-life violence. Is it scarier than violence in the movies or on TV?

Elementary School

Have the children discuss violence in the entertainment media and in real life. Is there a difference? Have copies of the daily newspaper available for the group. Have them find examples in the newspaper of real-life violence. Discuss the violence and its possible consequences. Have them discuss real-life violence with their parents.

Middle School

Have the group discuss violence in both the entertainment media and in real life. Is there a difference? Have them list examples of violence. Show a videotaped newscast. Discuss any violence that was shown or mentioned. What parts of the violent actions were not shown? How does violence in real life affect real people? Why is violence part of the news? Does the news report all of the consequences of violence? Does it show the effects on both the victim and the perpetrator? Have participants reflect in their journals on how violence in the news affects them.

High School

Discuss violence in the entertainment media and violence in real life. Is there a difference? Show the group a videotape of a local TV news program. Discuss the impact of violence on people's lives. Some TV stations have created family-friendly newscasts, in which they show fewer images of violent news stories. Have the group react to this idea. Have them analyze several different local TV news reports to categorize and time the stories. Discuss whether the different stations report the news differently. Call a local station and invite the news director (or other news professional) to visit the group and discuss the group's findings.

Review
Reflect
React

11. EXAMINE COMICS IN THE PRINT MEDIA

*More than 150 million Americans read the comics in some 1,500
newspapers every day, in addition to 200 million readers abroad
in more than 40 languages in 100 countries.*
                                    Scott Stamp Monthly, March 1996

CONCEPT:

Comics are appealing because of their simple and easily recognizable style and characters.
Comic strips in the newspapers are said to help sell the papers; they are not necessarily humor-
ous, and some perhaps should be called "slice of life" strips. Political cartoons are drawings that
typically scrutinize or satirize social or political issues. With newspaper and magazine audiences, they are reportedly more popular than are the editorials. Comics, including comic strips,
comic books, and political cartoons, can reflect current trends and should be analyzed as cultural icons.

ACTIVITIES:

Preschool - 1st Grade

Gather multiple copies of the Sunday newspaper comics section. Have children cut out
appealing and colorful cartoon characters and paste them on construction paper. Have
them explain the reasons for their choices. Then have them create and share new stories
about these characters.

Elementary School

Use multiple copies of the Sunday newspaper comics section. Each child should select one
comic strip, cut it out, paste it on construction paper, and "white-out" the dialog located
in the conversation bubbles. Then each is to write new dialog for the comic strip. Have
them share their strips and discuss why comic strips are so appealing.

Middle School

Have participants bring in comic books or visit a local comic book store. Analyze the covers, format, themes, heroes, super heroes, characters, plots, purpose, audience, ads, etc.
Discuss what themes seem to predominate. Have participants create new comic book
heroes or characters unlike those they have seen. Have a comic book enthusiast or col-
lector join the group and discuss the comic book genre and the new characters that were
created by the group.

High School

Have the teenagers collect political cartoons from books, magazines, and newspapers.
Ask them to create media journals with numerous political cartoons by the same
artist, analyzing them, and reflecting on the artist's approach to social issues.
Discuss how cartoonists use this medium to stimulate critical thinking. Have them
collect political cartoons on a given topic and discuss the various viewpoints. Each
participant is to select a social issue and create an original political cartoon to be
displayed and discussed in the group.

"REVIEW REFLECT REACT"

12. IDENTIFY "JOLTS"

That's how almost all the top American shows get their audiences.
They obey the First Law of Commercial Television: Thou shalt give
them enough jolts per minute (jpm's) or thou shalt lose them.
"The First Law of Commercial Television," by Morris Wolfe,
Mass Media and Popular Culture

CONCEPT:

A "jolt" in a movie, TV program, or commercial refers to an action – a "cut" (splice), a joke, or a shocking scene - that causes viewers to stay tuned. "Jolts per minute" is a term explaining the number of laugh lines, action shots, or sensational scenes within a 60-second period. The jolts per minute rate has been increasing, probably due to an increase in the use of remote control devices and a decrease in audience attention span. Cuts are multiple camera shots that have been edited together to create a music video, TV commercial, or other packaged media product.

ACTIVITIES:

Preschool - 1st Grade

Videotape and show several children's TV commercials. Teach the children to count the cuts in a 30-second TV ad. Compare the number of cuts in the commercials. Discuss the children's reactions to the fast-paced commercials. Why do they think creators of the ads use so many cuts?

Elementary School

Videotape and show a series of children's TV commercials. Teach the children to count the cuts in 30-second TV ads. Have the children create a fictitious product and develop a 30-second ad for it. Have them act out their ads for the group. Videotape their ads, if possible. View the ads and discuss ways they could be made more lively and interesting.

Middle School

Videotape a non-controversial music video that has many cuts. Show it to the group. Teach them to count the cuts in 30-second TV ads. Have them:
- Analyze the scene changes and camera angles;
- Discuss the purpose of the cuts;
- List the number of cuts in 10 TV commercials during the following week; and
- Determine the average number of seconds the image is on the screen during a typical 30-second ad.

Discuss their findings, their reactions to the cuts, and why there are so many cuts.

High School

Discuss the concept of "jolts per minute." Discuss the most annoying jolts. During their normal TV viewing the next week, have the participants list all the tactics used to keep viewers "glued" to their sets. Have them write daily journal entries after each day's TV viewing, reflecting on the techniques used to intentionally manipulate the audience. Combine the data they have collected in a chart or summary. Discuss discernible patterns.

13. LISTEN CRITICALLY

Here's what we must teach our children in the '90s - the skill of selective listening.

Jim Rohn, *The Treasury of Quotes*

CONCEPT:

Listening is a part of the communication process that functions even before we learn to read or write. It is an essential component of the language arts. A great deal of what we learn each day is acquired through listening. By becoming more adept listeners, we can better understand the world around us. Much of the experience of television and movies is contingent on listening. To listen critically is not an innate skill, but one that must be learned.

ACTIVITIES:

Preschool - 1st Grade

Play a listening game. Go behind a screen or door and make a noise. Have the children guess what that noise is. Then go behind the screen and talk to them each time with a different tone of voice such as happy, angry, sad, questioning, etc. Have the children interpret each tone of voice and discuss the differences.

Elementary School

Each time a sound filmstrip, videotape, or film is used in the group setting, discuss the background music. Talk about the style, purpose, and appeal. Discuss their reaction, why music has been added to the material and whether the music adds or detracts from the purpose of the presentation. Would they prefer to change the music? If so, in what way?

Middle School

Videotape numerous segments of television programs or movies containing dramatic background music. Play each segment to the group members with the TV turned around so the pictures cannot be viewed. Discuss the music and what type of scene it might accompany. Then watch the segment together and see how accurate their guesses were. Repeat for each segment. Discuss the role background music plays. Have the members listen to soundtracks from movies and guess what might be happening during various segments of the soundtracks.

High School

Have participants listen to a radio newscast. Discuss:
- What details were left out of each news story?
- What voice qualities or tones of voice added to or detracted from the message?
- Were there any examples of platitudes, emotionally charged words, or insincerity?

Have the participants create news stories and read them aloud with different dialects, tones of voice, inflections, etc. Analyze the impact of the different versions.

14. IDENTIFY SPECIAL EFFECTS

It may not surprise audiences to learn that all the rockets in 'Apollo 13' are models, digitally inserted in the picture. They may not suspect that the same is true of the city of Camelot in 'First Knight'...Effects have become so good that even trained observers often do not suspect they are seeing visual trickery.
The Houston Chronicle, July 23, 1995

CONCEPT:

Special effects add excitement and realism to the images in TV commercials and programs, video games, and movies. Through the use of editing techniques and computers, it is now possible to simulate any image, background, or action without enduring hazards. In media productions ranging from "Star Wars" to interactive virtual reality computer games, special effects are used to add authenticity. Message consumers have begun to take for granted the special effects in entertainment media, and are often disappointed if they are not spectacular. Special effects allow viewers to experience scenes or sensations that have never happened.

ACTIVITIES:

Preschool - 1st Grade

Show the children a videotaped TV commercial that contains special effects. Discuss whether what they saw could actually happen and whether it was exciting or interesting. Discuss whether the ad would have been as appealing without special effects.

Elementary School

Discuss special effects used in movies. Have the children list some examples from movies they have seen. Why were the special effects included? Have the children keep a log of special effects they see on TV or in movies over a one-week period. Discuss their findings and the purposes of any special effects they observed.

Middle School

Have participants watch a videotaped portion of a movie that contains special effects. Discuss whether the scenes could have actually happened in real life. Have the group make a composite list of special effects they would like to see in a movie. Discuss what would be needed to actually film the scenes.

High School

Discuss special effects in music videos. Videotape and show some music videos that contain images that have been manipulated by techniques such as "morphing." Discuss how those scenes were created. Invite a computer expert or television editor to visit the group and answer questions the teenagers have. Schedule a forum with panelists from the mass media and/or computer industry to discuss "Can you believe your eyes?" Invite the public and facilitate interaction.

15. EVALUATE MEDIA'S CONTENT SELECTION PROCESS

ABC...declined to carry President Bush's live address Wednesday night. Sherrie Rollins, head of ABC News' press department, said... 'We did not think it was newsworthy enough for live coverage.'

Rocky Mountain News, January 25, 1991

CONCEPT:

The process of determining what will be included in each media presentation is carried out by the "gatekeepers" – the decision makers. These people are responsible for the covers of books and magazines, the inclusion or exclusion of news stories, and the amount of space or time devoted to each news story. What we know about the world around us is often limited by the gatekeepers' subjective choices. Each mass medium uses specific criteria for the information it conveys and therefore defines the specific knowledge and perceptions delivered to its viewers, listeners, or readers.

ACTIVITIES:

Preschool - 1st Grade

Show the children a variety of picture books and talk about the covers. Discuss which covers are the most appealing, colorful, and eye-catching. Have each child select a book and state reasons for the selection. Explain that the publisher has chosen that cover for the book in order to attract readers. Discuss other covers.

Elementary School

Have all the children read the same news article from a kids' news publication, such as *Weekly Reader*. Tell them their job is to write a one-sentence summary of that story. Share their summaries. Have them discuss the reasons their sentences are not all alike. Talk about the personal judgment involved in the selection process. Discuss how the mass media are made up of individuals who make personal judgments regarding the information that is provided to the audiences.

Middle School

Collect various teen magazines. Have the group members analyze the subjects of articles. Discuss topics that are covered, ignored, recurring themes, photos, etc. What factors determine the choice of topics? Have each participant write a journal entry about the selection process.

High School

Have the participants collect newspaper editorials for a week. Discuss the topics. What other topics are important and could have been included? Discuss reasons why the editors might have selected these topics. Have participants ask the editor specific questions by phone, e-mail, or in person. Have them write journal entries about how the selection process used by the media affects the general populace.

16. RECOGNIZE ATTENTION-GETTING STRATEGIES

*In seeking the right sound, advertisers will use whatever works to pull you
into the commercial - even if the noises are less than pleasant.*
"Why You Watch Some Commercials - Whether You Mean To or Not"
TV Guide, February 20, 1988

CONCEPT:

Before any message is delivered to an audience, individuals must first be drawn in. The mass media struggle to capture the attention of the viewer, reader, or listener. The print and electronic media use many strategies to appeal to the audience. Billboards, for instance, seem to have a "2-second rule." If the message can't be comprehended in 2 seconds or less, the billboard is virtually ineffective. Magazine and newspaper ads, signs, TV and radio commercials, T-shirts, book covers, etc., all vie for consumer attention. Competition is the driving force behind all media techniques.

ACTIVITIES:

Preschool - 1st Grade

Have children bring numerous empty cereal boxes to the group meeting. Have the children compare and contrast the designs, colors, cartoon or animal characters, send-away items, contests, and TV commercials for the cereals. After discussing all of these features, have the children design a box for a new cereal, to include a name, a box design, colors, free gifts, a TV ad, etc.

Elementary School

Collect 10-15 picture books, some with enticing and colorful covers, and some with plain unappealing covers. Show these books to the children. Ask each child to choose a book. Discuss the choices that were made based on just the covers. Why are books with pretty or exciting covers more desirable? Discuss why publishers put attractive colorful covers on books. Have each child bring to the group a plain-covered book. Have the child carefully design and make a new interesting cover for the book. Have group members share their new covers and discuss their appeal.

Middle School

Have middle schoolers observe billboards, posters, and signs for one week. Discuss the most interesting and appealing ones. What specific things caught their attention? Why? Did everyone react the same way to these print messages? Compare and contrast two posters. What elements make a print message noticeable? As a group, create an attention-getting bulletin board or poster.

High School

Have participants focus on posters, signs, and billboards that catch their attention during a one-week period. Discuss why some capture their attention and some don't. Have each group member select a topic and create a message that is brief enough for a poster. Have a Design-a-Poster contest to create posters that spread important social messages, such as Don't Drink and Drive! After a period of time, interview people at random who have passed by the posters. Ask them which messages they remember and why. Is there a reason the poster layout or design captured their attention? Discuss the findings.

Review
Reflect   React

17. IDENTIFY MASS MEDIA'S MESSAGES AS "CONSTRUCTED" REALITY

In the real world, alcohol accounts for one-sixth or less of beverage use. In television's world, alcohol drinking occurs more often than the combined drinking of coffee, tea, soft drinks, and water.
George Gerbner, as quoted in *Psychology* by David G. Myers

CONCEPT:

The mass media are in the business of delivering messages. What is seen, heard, or read may not be reality, but merely a construction. Consider the content of a print ad. Every component of that ad has been created, or constructed, for a specific purpose. The same is true in the entertainment industry and even the news industry. The TV news reports of an ongoing war are not the actual war, but selected images meant to convey the war to the viewers. By recognizing that the sounds and images have been selected to achieve a specific purpose, viewers become less gullible.

ACTIVITIES:

Preschool - 1st Grade

Show a short segment from a children's TV program. Ask whether people created the TV show or whether this was just a taped portion from real life. Have children think about a new TV show. Make up some main characters. What might happen? Where would it take place? Would this be a constructed program or real life? Discuss the fact that many TV shows are created for entertainment and are not real.

Elementary School

Collect newspapers to use with the group. Have children look at the photos in the papers and discuss them. Have each child select one photo. Discuss whether each photo is the whole story or a representation of the story. Could someone with a camera have been there and taken a different photo? Could that change the perceptions of the newspaper reader? Select one newspaper photo and have all the children interpret that photo. Discuss how a photographer constructs reality.

Middle School

Have participants assume the role of producers of a TV show entitled "A Day in the Life of a _____" (Principal, Teenager, Housewife, Shopper, Dog, etc.). Consider components such as: location, costumes, lighting, scene changes, props, activities, dialog, point-of-view, purpose, audience, etc. Discuss how these elements can affect the final presentation. Discuss the reality they are constructing. Have them write journal entries reflecting on the reality of messages they get from the mass media.

High School

Have the group choose one local scene that will represent their town or city on a postcard. After making the selection, talk about how the photo should be taken to advertise the area. Consider factors such as: time of the day, season of the year, people or animals to be included, activities, lighting, costumes, props, etc. After determining all of the elements that might enhance the photo, compare this to the actual unenhanced scene. Discuss the concept of constructing reality.

18. DE-CONSTRUCT ALL MEDIA MESSAGES

The point is that the producers of media 'construct' their product, whether it is the 6 o'clock news, a TV drama, your daily newspaper, a magazine ad, or a record album, to create illusions or to make a world that is exciting and entertaining enough to keep audiences interested.

Mass Media and Popular Culture

CONCEPT:

Media literacy cannot be achieved until techniques have been learned for de-constructing the messages of the mass media. Analyzing all of the components that together constitute a political ad, for instance, helps the consumer understand the purpose, content, and impact of the final product. The typical message is not a random or chance composite, but is intricately planned and created to leave a specific impression. All media messages are constructions.

ACTIVITIES:

Preschool - 1st Grade

Collect and display the containers that toys are packaged in. Discuss the various components of the packages: colors, photographs, drawings, words, characters, etc. Talk about why these specific elements are part of each package design. Brainstorm an idea for a new toy. Have the children design its package, considering all of the components that were discussed.

Elementary School

Select posters to use as discussion starters. Discuss the various components of each poster, including people, animals, background, props, message, etc. Why were these particular components chosen? Have children work in small groups to modify an existing poster to alter its impact. Discuss the impact of each newly constructed poster.

Middle School

Have the group view an educational video, such as a National Geographic or Discovery Channel TV program. Discuss the opening, background music, voice-overs, setting, actors, clothing, lighting, props, etc. How do these different elements affect the final product? Discuss what would happen if there was a change in one element, such as the voice-over. By using a young child's voice or that of a person with a distinctive accent, how would the perceptions of the viewers be altered? Make a list of the key components that are important aspects of the final product. Use the list for future discussions when de-constructing other media messages.

High School

Have the teenagers de-construct magazine ads, considering various components, such as people, animals, clothing, background, lighting, props, text, camera angle, color, white space, etc. Ask small groups to select topics for PSAs that deal with a relevant social issue, such as "Drugs Kill!" Using the same components they studied, have them create the layout for a magazine ad that promotes the chosen PSA topic. Place the ads in a student publication and observe their impact by interviewing readers.

19. ASSESS THE ACCURACY, FAIRNESS, AND ETHICS OF MASS MEDIA INFORMATION

Get your facts first, and then you can distort them as much as you please.

Mark Twain

CONCEPT:

Electronic media, print media, and the Internet constitute the communication tools of the information society. In fact, most of what is known about the world around us comes from the mass media. To question the facts or attitudes of the mass media involves reviewing, reflecting, and reacting. To test the accuracy, fairness, or ethics of the messages of any medium necessitates critical thinking and additional insight from other sources.

ACTIVITIES:

Preschool - 1st Grade

Place on a chalkboard or poster some accurate statements, along with some, such as "the sun is purple," that the children will recognize as inaccurate. Read aloud each statement to the children, discussing whether or not each is true. Discuss whether something is true just because it is written or spoken. How do they know whether it is true or not? Talk about the importance of learning about things for themselves instead of just automatically accepting claims made by other people.

Elementary School

Create a list of age-appropriate facts - some accurate and some not (e.g., Columbus discovered America in 1942) - and distribute the list to the children. Have them do research to find out the accuracy of each statement. Discuss the concept that something can be printed and still not be true. How do the children think they would react if untrue statements were written about them? Discuss how inaccurate and unfair statements can hurt people.

Middle School

Have the participants learn the definitions of these words: accurate, biased, ethical. Have them discuss what would happen if something untrue were circulated about them. How might this affect a political candidate, for example? Discuss tabloid news sources. Make tabloid newspapers available and have small groups of participants analyze the content of these publications. Have each group select one fact and do research to prove whether it is accurate. Discuss the process used to determine the accuracy of these statements.

High School

Discuss ethics, bias, fairness, and accuracy. Discuss how these concepts relate to the mass media. Have each participant create fictitious and damaging headlines that might impact readers. Share the headlines and discuss their potential effects. Discuss the long-term impact of inaccurate, unfair, biased, or unethical statements in the media. Have them reflect in journals about this topic.

Review
Reflect
React

20. EXAMINE THE MASS MEDIA'S INFLUENCE ON THINKING, ATTITUDES, AND BEHAVIOR

In 1989, when '60 Minutes' described the alleged health dangers of the pesticide Alar, panicked millions stopped eating apples.
"The Truth About TV News," *Reader's Digest*, November, 1993

CONCEPT:

The mass media can influence the general population in a myriad of ways, from shaping the outcomes of political elections to determining which athletic shoes are "hot." Humor trends, for example, are cultural constructions that evolve from the presentations of comedians, movies, comics, and sitcoms that are popular with the masses. Appropriate thinking of society (political correctness) may be another construction of mass media. One's identity is often the result of standards internalized from many media messages. Individuality often necessitates countering these messages.

ACTIVITIES:

Preschool - 1st Grade

Show videotaped food commercials from kidvid (children's TV programming). Have the children pretend they have arrived from another planet and, based on the ads, determine the usual or normal diet for kids on Earth. Ask them what their reactions would be if they saw a TV ad for asparagus as a snack food. Discuss how TV ads influence their personal requests for specific foods.

Elementary School

Discuss the children's favorite brands of athletic shoes. Compose a list of the top three. Discuss why these brands are so popular. Are the shoe designs based on market research? Is one design better than another? Have the children create and conduct a survey that reveals which athletic shoes are favored and why. Analyze and discuss the survey findings.

Middle School

Have the participants create and conduct a survey about favorite soft drinks. Tally the results. Why are the winners so popular? Is it taste or advertising? Conduct a blind taste test, using the top three drinks from the survey results. Have the subject attempt to name the brand after each taste. Discuss the taste test's results. Have the group brainstorm a new soft drink and suggest strategies they could use to make it as popular as the top three.

High School

Have the group members research the purpose of a public relations firm. Find out whether any company, group, or individual in the community uses the services of a PR firm. Invite a public relations professional to the group for an open discussion about the advantages and disadvantages of the PR field. Have small groups create an image for a fictitious person or company and develop strategies for getting that image out to the public. Have the group members reflect in their journals about the influence of public relations efforts.

21. CLASSIFY CELEBRITIES

Time makes heroes but dissolves celebrities.

Daniel Boorstin in *Parade*

CONCEPT:

A celebrity is someone widely known or recognized. As the result of celebrity status, the "celebrity du jour" often adorns magazine covers, authors best-selling books, and appears in TV commercials. Current lists of America's most influential people may include names such as Oprah Winfrey, Michael Jordan, or Jay Leno. These entertainment figures are certainly recognizable, but they are not necessarily societal leaders. Determining whether someone who is a celebrity should be a role model takes critical thinking – an essential part of media literacy training.

ACTIVITIES:

Preschool - 1st Grade

Place pictures of recognizable people, animals, or cartoon characters on a poster or bulletin board. Discuss who they are and why the children recognize them. Introduce and discuss the concept celebrity. Read a short story to the children about a real well-known person. Discuss why the person is well-known.

Elementary School

Show pictures of people, animals, or cartoon characters that most children recognize. Talk about the meaning of celebrity. Is Mickey Mouse a celebrity? How about Babe Ruth? Have the children talk through the requirements for someone to be a celebrity. Does the term necessarily mean a good person? Have children explain their answers. With the aid of a dictionary, come to a group consensus about the meaning of celebrity. Based on the consensus, could a classmate be a celebrity? Can a dog be a celebrity? Discuss current examples of celebrities together with reasons for such status.

Middle School

Have participants create a list of celebrities. Then have them attempt to define celebrity status. Read aloud the definition from a dictionary. Discuss whether someone they know could become a celebrity. Is a celebrity always a noteworthy person? A good person? Have the group members create a "Celebrity of the Week" poster, with a picture and the reason for notoriety.

High School

Have young adults study numerous celebrities. What pressures do these people face because of their status? Have the youth determine how different individuals have responded to these pressures, both positively and negatively. Discuss whether a celebrity can have any semblance of a normal life. Create a list of recent celebrities who have been well-known for a short while before disappearing from the public eye. Have each participant write to a current celebrity or find printed interviews asking about the advantages and disadvantages of celebrity status.

22. IDENTIFY HEROES

The hero reveals the possibilities of human nature; the celebrity reveals the possibilities of the media.

Daniel Boorstin, *The Image*

CONCEPT:

Heroes can be real or fictional. The characteristics of heroes are diverse, but often include such features as overcoming adversity, supporting the underdog, performing unusual or compassionate feats, or standing up for what's right. Throughout history, there have been heroes, but they have not always been well-known. Examining the qualities that constitute heroics can help distinguish the true heroes from among the celebrities in our popular culture. The critical thinking required to differentiate between a celebrity (see previous page) and a hero can help young people identify their role models and thus affect their futures.

ACTIVITIES:

Preschool - 1st Grade

Read aloud to the children a picture book, such as *The Hole in the Dike* (retold by Norma Green and illustrated by Eric Carle), that contains a heroic figure. Discuss what makes the character a hero. Place this word on a bulletin board or a poster and list the names of other heroes the children suggest. Add to the list as warranted.

Elementary School

Discuss the concepts of celebrity and hero. Have the children use reference materials, such as a dictionary or encyclopedia, to learn more about these words. Place these words on a bulletin board or posterboard and have the children list candidates for each, based on the definitions they learned. Compare and contrast the celebrities and heroes listed. What generalizations can they make as a result of this discussion?

Middle School

Have each person bring pictures of people who are in the news, along with information about why they are newsworthy. Ask whether any are heroes. Discuss the concept of hero. Have them research this word in various reference materials, looking for specific qualities and examples. Have them interview parents, teachers, and other significant adults to learn about their personal heroes. Have the group summarize the findings and create a bulletin board showing pictures of heroes.

High School

Discuss the concepts of celebrity and hero. Research definitions and examples of these words. Make a list of people for each category, considering people from history as well as fictional, contemporary, and cartoon characters. Invite community leaders to a panel discussion, Celebrities vs. Heroes. Allow them to have an open dialog with the participants about characteristics of each. Have participants each write a journal entry entitled, "My Hero."

RESOURCES:

"Heroes," an interdisciplinary unit. Teacher Created Materials, Inc. (See Additional Resources section)

23. BECOME VISUALLY LITERATE

Beauty is altogether in the eye of the beholder.
General Lew Wallace

CONCEPT:

Visual literacy refers to the knowledge and skills needed to question, analyze, interpret, and evaluate images and print messages. It covers such areas as photographic techniques, layout, use of color, and computer-generated images. The visual components of any message must be de-constructed to ascertain potential impact and effectiveness. Visual literacy training is often relegated to art or photography classes, but it is an essential element of thinking critically about all media messages, and therefore must be integrated into all subject areas.

ACTIVITIES:

Preschool - 1st Grade

Read aloud a favorite picture book, sharing the illustrations with the children. Have each child choose one special illustration from the book and discuss why it is appealing. Have the group analyze one specific illustration, discussing the style, colors, point of view, action, realism, detail, etc. Repeat this activity often.

Elementary School

Provide a simple print drawing, such as a page from a coloring book, for each of the children. The goal is for them to use art materials (paint, crayons, construction paper, fabric, etc.) to complete the page so it is unique and interesting. Share the final products with the group, and discuss the differences and the techniques used. Discuss what image-makers do to create unusual and appealing print messages.

Middle School

Collect magazine ads that might appeal to or provoke teenagers. Place each ad on a piece of construction paper. Use the ads to instigate discussions about de-constructing the messages. Analyze various components of each ad, including color, layout, text, people or animals pictured, realism, appeal, audience, etc. Discuss these ads to determine which are the most effective for specific audiences.

High School

Have participants study photos in newspapers, yearbooks, or books by famous photographers. Analyze the purpose, impact, and selection of these photos. Invite a photojournalist to visit the group to answer questions about photojournalism as a career. Why are some pictures worth a thousand words? Give participants a photojournalism project: using 35mm cameras, they are to select and photograph appropriate scenes or people to make statements about relevant social issues. Display and discuss the photos. Arrive at a consensus concerning the importance of photos in the news industry.

RESOURCES:

MS & HS: "The Power of Newsprint," Lynne Meena videotape (see Additional Resources section)

HS: "Slim Hopes," Dr. Jeanne Kilbourne videotape (see Additional Resources section)

24. DISTINGUISH BETWEEN RELEVANT AND IRRELEVANT INFORMATION

Search 50 million web pages!

America Online, August, 1996

CONCEPT:

The volume of information is increasing at a staggering pace. People cannot retain all of the facts they are exposed to. Critical thinking requires an ongoing selection process that gives attention to the relevant and eliminates the irrelevant. What is relevant is by definition a subjective matter because it depends on such factors as experience, values, personality, interests, career, and circumstances at any given time. Some criteria for relevancy must be established in order to have a starting place for the selection process.

ACTIVITIES:

Preschool - 1st Grade

Help the children plan a group interview with an adult. Talk about what information is going to be important. Will they be able to learn everything about that adult? Create a list of topics they'll want to explore. Discuss their selection of specific questions to ask. Have them as a group interview an adult. Discuss the information they obtained from the interview.

Elementary School

Distribute a long list of facts to the children for them to read, or read it aloud to the group. Then have them attempt to remember specific facts from the list. Discuss the concept that the amount of information is increasing and that no one can learn it all. However, each person can learn how to find needed information. Invite a librarian or school library media specialist to visit the group to discuss relevant and irrelevant information. Have children interview the guest.

Middle School

Have the youth view a video or TV program on an important topic. Give them a test covering some very irrelevant facts that were in the program. Discuss the participants' reactions to the test. Can one person absorb all the information presented? Does anyone need it all? Have the group discuss some criteria for retaining relevant information about the topic. View the same program again and have them take notes about the relevant information. Have them compare notes and discuss the process for selecting relevant information.

High School

Discuss the many sources of information. Have the youth spend time on the Internet discovering the myriad of possibilities for gathering data. Discuss both relevant and irrelevant information that is available. Have each small group select a topic and create a list of relevant questions they would need to answer in order to write a report about the topic. Have the groups research the topics, share relevant information, and discuss what makes each fact relevant. Have group members discuss irrelevant data sources they encountered and why these were rejected.

25. DETERMINE POINT OF VIEW

*Luke, you're going to find that many of the truths we
cling to depend greatly on our own point of view.*
Obi-Wan-Kenobi, "Star Wars: Return of the Jedi"

CONCEPT:

Point of view (POV) refers to the viewpoint of the creator, author, director, character, or even the camera operator in media presentations. The newspaper editorial, in which the point of view is quite apparent, is an excellent example. However, in other situations the point of view is less obvious but may be just as influential. In movies, commercials, and TV shows, the camera can assume the position of the speaker or of any other member of the cast and thereby take a non-neutral role. One must examine whose viewpoint is represented and whether the piece is therefore slanted or opinionated. Determining the POV can help the individual better understand exactly whose story is being told.

ACTIVITIES:

Preschool - 1st Grade

Discuss opinions and why people can have different opinions about the same thing. Ask who likes sweet potatoes. Some children do and some don't. The same is true of a wide variety of other foods, colors, toys, games, etc. Explain that having a viewpoint does not mean that everyone who disagrees is wrong. Spend time teaching appreciation of others' ideas, preferences, opinions, and feelings.

Elementary School

Read aloud *The Pain and the Great One* by Judy Blume. Discuss the point of view of each of the two characters in the story. Have the children write a paragraph about a brother or sister or friend. Have each one read the paragraph aloud and then discuss its point of view. Read aloud books with different points of view, such as *Jack and the Beanstalk; The Beanstalk Incident* by Tim Paulson. Discuss the points of view.

Middle School

Have group members study editorials in the newspaper. Discuss how people can have different ideas about the same facts. Introduce the point of view concept. Have the group choose a topic that is somewhat controversial, such as whether middle school students should be allowed to leave the school grounds at lunchtime. Have each member of the group write a persuasive essay expressing a personal point of view.

High School

Introduce the concept of point of view. If it is an election year:
- Study political campaign ads and discuss the point of view in each one.
- Determine the number of actual issues that form the focus of the campaign.
- List the known points of view of each candidate.
- Determine what voting group each candidate is appealing to.

If it's not an election year:
- Have each student create a fictional political candidate.
- Write a 30-second radio ad from the point of view of the candidate.
- Tape the ads and then play them for the group.
- Discuss the point of view of each ad.

Ask participants to summarize how the use of point of view by the mass media can create or modify public opinion.

Review
Reflect
React

26. EXAMINE THE PORTRAYAL OF SOCIETAL GROUPS

Only about 20 percent of all characters on children's commercial television are female.

Susan Douglas, as quoted in the *Nashville Banner*,
February 28, 1996

CONCEPT:

What the general population knows about the world around them is continually being shaped by the mass media. Specific population subsets, such as the disabled, the elderly, teenagers, ethnic groups, etc., have minimum representation in this world view. Therefore, the groups most often portrayed appear to be the most important. As the media depict an increased number of these subsets, the diversity of our culture is more accurately portrayed. It is necessary to examine, analyze, and evaluate the media's portrayal of all people groups in our culture.

ACTIVITIES:

Preschool - 1st Grade

Have the children discuss the most familiar population groups (subsets), such as children, elderly, ethnic groups, and disabled. Help them broaden their ideas by showing pictures of other subsets. Have them bring catalogs and print ads to the next group meeting. Have the children look through the catalogs and ads to find representatives of each group mentioned. Discuss their impressions and any resulting generalizations.

Elementary School

Discuss population subsets in our culture, such as children, teenagers, disabled, ethnic groups, etc. Using the Sunday comics from the local newspaper, have the children work in small groups to find comic strip characters to represent each of the groups. Discuss their findings, their frustrations, and the generalizations they develop.

Middle School

Discuss the diverse groups that make up our culture, such as ethnic groups, age-related groups, disabled, etc. Create a composite list of the groups. Have the participants spend one week analyzing all of the TV commercials they see, keeping track of the various subsets represented in the commercials. Discuss their findings and have them write letters that summarize their views. Have them send the letters to program sponsors or a local TV station.

High School

Discuss the many population groups in our culture. Analyze the representation of these subsets in TV sitcoms. List specific TV sitcoms and the group(s) portrayed. Invite representatives from all possible population subsets to a panel discussion about the accuracy of TV's portrayal of society. Invite community members to be in the audience. Have an open discussion about the impact of TV on society's attitudes (acceptance or rejection) toward members of specific subsets. Have participants reflect in their journals about these interactions.

27. DISTINGUISH BETWEEN FORM AND CONTENT

The medium is the message.
Marshall McLuhan

CONCEPT:

There are two components of any media message: form and content. Form refers to the format or medium, such as billboard, music video, movie, etc. Content refers to the actual text, images, sound, and substance of the message. By distinguishing between form and content, the message consumer can separate the message from the delivery mode and recognize the power of the various communications devices.

ACTIVITIES:

Preschool - 1st Grade

Have the children list and discuss the various ways a message can be sent: TV, newspaper, book, poster, radio, etc. Ask whether it matters which way a message is sent. Have them explain their answers. Discuss the content of a picture book and whether the content changes if the same story appears in the newspaper.

Elementary School

Have the group decide on an important message, such as "don't play with matches," that children everywhere should know. After they select their message, list the many ways that message could be sent. Talk about the different types of formats. Have them choose the best way to reach other elementary-age children. Now have each child write a review of a current movie to send to other children. Should the movie review be in a different format than the safety message? Discuss reasons.

Middle School

Distribute newspapers and have each participant select a newspaper ad. Discuss the form and content of the ads. Discuss what would be different if the form were changed. Discuss what would be different if the content were changed. Have each participant take the selected ad and modify the content. Display the new ads and discuss their appropriate audience and expected impact.

High School

Talk about both form and content. Have participants do research on Marshall McLuhan and his influence on the field of communications. Have each participant write an essay to explain and react to McLuhan's statement, "The medium is the message." Discuss this topic and its many ramifications on society.

28. DEFINE TV GENRE

Since commercial television is aimed at a mass audience, there is a need for a variety of types of programming to attract as any people as possible.

Mass Media and Popular Culture

CONCEPT:

The television experience is made up of many categories: sitcoms, newscasts, movies, cartoons, soap operas, sports, commercials, etc. Each category can have a different appeal and a different impact. For instance, one could not compare the influence of a music video to a weather report. The audience may have distinct expectations from one TV format to another. There may be many dissimilarities even within the same genre. For example, not all cartoons have equal impact. One major step towards media literacy is understanding the dynamic influence of television and the existence of diverse aspects that make this a pervasive and powerful medium.

ACTIVITIES:

Preschool - 1st Grade

Have the children name as many different TV programs as possible and group them into categories such as cartoons, sports, movies, etc. Have them create a label for each category. Discuss the categories and the differences among them. Talk about other categories that did not get mentioned, such as commercials, news, nature shows, etc.

Elementary School

Have children discuss favorite TV shows. Have them work in small groups to create as many different categories for their TV experiences as they can. Discuss these labels and create one master list, that can be added to over time. Have the children keep a copy of the list of categories. Every time they watch TV, they should refer to the list and label each program. Discuss their findings including which type they watch most often, etc. Discuss whether all categories affect them the same way.

Middle School

Discuss TV categories, listing examples of each. Give copies of a local television viewing schedule to each group of participants. Have them analyze the many TV listings, noting the number of different categories that are offered, the most popular genre, the time slots for the different categories, and whether some cable networks specialize in certain types of programming. Discuss their findings. Have them write journal entries with their reflections on the variety of TV offerings.

High School

Discuss the many different types of TV experiences available through broadcast and cable TV. Research the Nielsen ratings system. Have small groups of participants create surveys to discover individual preferences, expectations, and impacts of each category. Have them conduct these surveys over a one-week period. Discuss their findings. Compare the published list of the most-watched TV shows of the week with their survey findings. What conclusions can be drawn about various programs, their popularity, and their impact?

29. DETERMINE THE ROLE OF PRINT MEDIA

To base thought only on speech is to try nailing whispers to the wall. Writing freezes thought and offers it up for inspection.
Jack Rosenthal, *New York Times Magazine*

CONCEPT:

A print mass medium uses technology and reaches a large number of people. Print media include books, magazines, newspapers, advertising fliers, billboards, brochures, and other forms of static messages. Even messages that are printed on clothing must be considered part of this medium. Each of the print formats serves a specific purpose. There has been a concern that news services available through other media, such as the Internet or 24-hour TV news channels, will replace newspapers. That does not appear to be happening. Newspapers are important not merely because of their content but also because of their format. Print media compete with electronic media for our time and money but, due to their static nature, print messages can be more easily accessed, studied, and evaluated.

ACTIVITIES:

Preschool - 1st Grade

Have children bring examples of "environmental print" (i.e. cereal boxes, ads, books, etc.) to the group setting. After collecting a large number, have them sort and label them. Discuss the different groups of print materials and why they are all necessary. Which is the most appealing? What types do they have in their homes?

Elementary School

Have children list as many examples of print formats as they can. Discuss the differences between them. Discuss the reason some messages are in book form and others are in magazines or newspapers. Discuss which of these formats might be the best for advertising an upcoming local concert, explaining the causes of earthquakes, giving the schedule of next week's TV programs, printing the text of the President's inaugural speech, or summarizing U.S. history for 5th-grade students.

Middle School

Have the participants list the various print message formats. Involve them in a discussion of the advantages and disadvantages of each of the print media. Have them bring in examples of magazines, advertising fliers, newspapers, books, catalogs, comic books, etc. Discuss the purpose of each format. Discuss the role of books in our society. Have each person create a list of "Books Too Good To Miss" and share them with the group. Discuss what society would be like without free access to books.

High School

Define print media. Have participants study the various print media for several weeks, listing the purpose and audience of each format. Then have them work in small groups to create top ten lists of various print genre such as comic book characters, books for the college-bound, magazines, mystery books, etc. Discuss and share the lists.

30. EVALUATE THE ROLE OF ELECTRONIC MEDIA

The average child watches 1,689 minutes of television per week.
"Facts About Television," *TV-Free America*

CONCEPT:

The electronic mass media include television, radio, CDs, videotapes, computers, audio cassettes, video games, and other formats that use electronic technology and reach large audiences. Each of these formats has both advantages and disadvantages, fulfills a distinct role, and is designed for a specific purpose and for a specific audience. The electronic media now have a greater impact on our culture than ever before, as the technology encompasses such developments as multimedia applications and broadcast fax. The resulting communication is so immediate and diverse that the role of the electronic media must be evaluated.

ACTIVITIES:

Preschool - 1st Grade

Introduce the topic of television and why it is important in our lives. List different ways it is used in the children's homes. Discuss what life would be like without TV. In what ways might the children's lives be better? In what ways might their lives be worse? Is TV more important than playing, talking, or visiting with relatives? Discuss.

Elementary School

Define electronic media. Have the children make a list of all the electronic media they can name. Have them do research about each medium on the list and share their findings. Discuss what life was like for families 100 years ago without these media. Have the children write stories or draw pictures about a typical day 100 years ago. Share and discuss their work. Are there children in the world now who don't have electronic media? Discuss what their life is like.

Middle School

Define electronic media. Make a list of various types of electronic media. What is the role and advantage of each? Ask each participant to create a survey to ask teenagers and adults to select the most important electronic medium and how much time they spend in a typical week with that medium. Those surveyed should provide reasons for their choices. Chart and discuss the group's findings. Publish the survey findings in the school or organization newspaper or other publications.

High School

Define electronic media and share examples. Make a communications timeline, with each participant researching information about an invention, such as the telegraph, television, computer, fax machine, etc. Predict some changes in communications that may occur in the next 10, 20, and 50 years. Have them write entries in their journals about these predictions. Discuss the role of the electronic media in their personal lives and in a democratic society. How do their ideas compare with media analysts and other experts in the media field, such as Michael Medved in *Hollywood Vs America* or Neil Postman in *Amusing Ourselves to Death*?

31. COMPARE/CONTRAST HARD AND SOFT NEWS

On September 20, 1995, "on KPRC TV in Houston, a full 37% of the news is judged trivial."
"Pavlov's TV Dogs," Rocky Mountain Media Watch

CONCEPT:

"Hard" news refers to factual information, data, and statistics, including the serious and vital news stories. "Soft" news is the non-essential content such as celebrity stories, features, columns, comic strips, and human interest stories covered in newspapers, TV news programs, and news magazines. Although hard news is the essence of the news industry, ratings and circulation expectations cause an increasing amount of soft news stories to be included. The news industry serves the public as an important source of vital information. However, as audiences gravitate toward stories covering food, entertainment, advice, travel, and consumer reports, soft news infiltrates more of the news media.

ACTIVITIES:

Preschool - 1st Grade

Read aloud a picture book about newspapers such as *The Furry News: How to Make a Newspaper* by Loreen Leedy. Ask which children get a newspaper at home. Have those children who get a newspaper at home ask their parents what they like best about the newspaper. Get a copy of a popular local newspaper and talk about the different sections.

Elementary School

Read aloud a book about the newspaper industry, such as *Newspapers* (A New True Book). Supply one newspaper to each child and have them look through the sections of the newspaper, studying the different features. Discuss hard news and soft news. Have the children divide news clippings into two piles: hard news and soft news. Discuss why a newspaper contains both types of news.

Middle School

Discuss hard news and soft news. Invite a journalist to visit the group to discuss what makes the news each day, and why soft news is included. Analyze a local newspaper, categorizing the various components as soft news and hard news. Have each group member create and conduct a survey to learn what parts of the newspaper adults like best. Discuss their findings.

High School

Have the group view portions of TV tabloid news programs, such as "Hard Copy" or "Entertainment Tonight." Discuss the content. Is this news? Have participants explain their answers. What is news? Construct a group definition. Is everything that happens worthy of being reported in the news? What content criteria should be used? Have them write letters, send e-mail messages to the tabloid producers or find published analyses to learn about their selection criteria. Share the responses that are received.

RESOURCES:

"Creating Critical TV Viewers," video and guide (see Additional Resources section)

32. REFLECT ON ECONOMICS - THE DRIVING FORCE BEHIND THE MASS MEDIA

In terms of dollars, 1995 was the most successful year in U. S. movie history, with more than $5.4 billion generated by movies in theatrical release.

The Seattle Times, January 28, 1996

CONCEPT:

The purpose of most mass media efforts is to make money. With few exceptions, the driving force behind the media is to create revenue. This is a concept that must be recognized in order to withstand the persuasiveness and built-in bias of advertising, movies, broadcast and cable TV, radio, the print media, etc. The news industry, for example, does not represent pure journalism. Advertisers, ratings, circulation, and other pressures influence the content of the news. The gatekeepers (decision makers) and their motivations must be understood to become a media literate citizen.

ACTIVITIES:

Preschool - 1st Grade

Discuss why books, movies, comic books, CDs and tapes, newspapers, and other entertainment and information sources are not free. Why do people have to pay for these items? What if the books at a bookstore were free? Discuss some of the expenses involved in these businesses and why there must be a cost.

Elementary School

Allow children to speculate about who pays for programs on broadcast TV. Have them list the expenses involved in making a TV program. Ask who pays these expenses. Discuss the role of sponsors. Talk about public television and how its programs are paid for, including fund raisers, government funding, and corporate sponsors. Have each child select one TV program to watch, with the assignment to list all of the sponsors of that show. Discuss the sponsors and their role.

Middle School

Discuss the content that is broadcast on several radio stations. Have participants define and discuss "niche marketing." Have them do an analysis of sponsors on local radio stations at various times of the day. Compare findings. Invite a marketing professional from a local radio station to visit the group to answer questions about the relationship between economics and the radio industry. Have participants reflect in their journals about a career in marketing.

High School

Have each small group member do research on one mass medium. Discuss the purpose and size of audience of the medium they selected. Have them research the costs of advertising, such as a full page ad in the newspaper, 30 seconds of air time on the radio, 30 seconds of air time on local TV, etc. Research ad costs during a major television event, such as the Olympics or the Super Bowl. What was the total revenue from the ads? Why are the ad costs so high? Invite various media representatives to visit and discuss the impact advertisers have on their work. Have participants write journal entries on this topic.

33. ASSESS THE POWER OF IMAGES

An ounce of image is worth a pound of performance.
                                                    Dr. Laurence J. Peter

CONCEPT:

Image is defined in *Webster's New Collegiate Dictionary* as a "reproduction or imitation of the form of a person or thing." Images are everywhere! Advertising uses images to persuade and manipulate. For example, the power of images can be seen in the people who emulate the media's standards of beauty or appearance. The results can be helpful or detrimental, depending on how realistic the standards are. Becoming aware of images and evaluating their impact are components of media literacy.

ACTIVITIES:

Preschool - 1st Grade

Discuss what we mean when we say someone is pretty or handsome. Do different people have different ideas about this? Spend time discussing personal opinions and individual standards. Show magazine ads and discuss whether the people are good-looking Do the images tell us anything about the people? Are some qualities more important than looks? Have the children explain their answers.

Elementary School

Have children bring in catalogs and magazine ads that contain images of people. Talk about how all people have ideas about what they want to look like. Have the children find pictures and words that describe their appearance now and in the future. Have each child create a collage of images and words that represent them. Are the children able to find images that adequately represent their appearance? If not, discuss the reasons, such as, the variety of images is too limited.

Middle School

Sometimes the images portrayed in the media affect our perceptions of people. Select one person who is often in the news. Have the group members bring in different photos from magazines or newspapers picturing that individual. Display the photos and discuss which ones are flattering and which ones are not. How can the image of a person affect the reaction of the reader or viewer? Discuss the power of images presented via the mass media.

High School

Discuss the power of images. Show a school yearbook and discuss flattering and unflattering photos. Analyze magazine ads' power to define standards of beauty such as, pretty, handsome, rugged, etc. How realistic are these images? Do these images affect the participants' standards for acceptable looks? Draw a picture of a "typical" teen as depicted in the media. Discuss the impact that models and other "beautiful people" have on the participants' lives and self-concepts. Invite a model to the group to talk about how beauty is "constructed." Have students reflect in their journals about the power of mass media images.

REVIEW
REFLECT
REACT

RESOURCES:

Reviving Ophelia, Dr. Mary Pipher (see Additional Resources section)

34. INVESTIGATE THE COMPUTER'S ROLE IN SOCIETY

For the first time, American consumers are buying more personal computers than televisions.

Rocky Mountain News, April 30, 1996

CONCEPT:

Computers have revolutionized such functions as the management of information and the development of entertainment media. Some tasks are extremely complex or impossible without the use of a computer, such as, electronic mail, graphics design, information analysis, etc. Computers are used extensively by a large percentage of the population, including children, who play games, compose reports, and access information. The Internet, a worldwide network of computer-delivered information, expands the computer's role into previously unforeseen areas. Because any technology can be used for good or evil, critical thinking about the use and potential misuse of computers is essential.

ACTIVITIES:

Preschool - 1st Grade

Discuss what a computer is. List uses of computers. Read aloud an introductory book about computers, such as *Kermit Learns How Computers Work*. Ask which children have used computers. Create an ongoing computer job list adding new jobs that computers can do for us. Discuss the many ways computers help us.

Elementary School

Invite adults to visit the group on different occasions. Have each one discuss how computers help on the job. Discuss what the jobs were like before there were computers. Have the children draw pictures of the visitors with their computers on the job, with captions explaining how the computers are used.

Middle School

Research the history of computers. Have a qualified person open an unplugged computer and let everyone look inside. Invite a computer programmer or analyst to visit the group to discuss how computers have altered our society. Have each participant visit an adult at the worksite and see how computers are used on the job. Have each person reflect in a journal entry about how that job would be different without the use of a computer.

High School

Have the teenagers research recent writings about new uses of computers in medicine, sports, entertainment media, etc. Discuss what tasks computers do best. Predict what computers might be doing in 5, 10, or 20 years. Discuss the Internet. Have them explore options on the Internet, such as reference materials, web pages, news services, stock market updates, etc. Have them write letters to their ancestors about what computers are and how they benefit society.

35. SELECT APPROPRIATE STANDARDS FOR VIEWING, LISTENING, AND READING

A misplaced pursuit of democracy, a particularly American failing, may help to explain why some parents have such difficulties controlling television.
The Plug-In Drug

CONCEPT:

The myriad of messages available each day through the media contain the entire range of "the good, the bad, and the ugly." Each individual must select appropriate choices for both information and entertainment. This is not a censorship issue, but is one dealing with interests, standards, and personal taste. Recognizing that not all media messages are equally worthy of one's time is an important concept for young people to grasp. For example, adopting a "selectavision" approach - always searching for the best that TV has to offer – allows television to be utilized in a positive and appropriate way.

ACTIVITIES:

Preschool - 1st Grade

Take children to a library and talk about the large selection of books available. Ask the children if all the books are appropriate for them. Discuss how they can make choices about the books they want, considering such things as the covers, content, or the section of the library. Discuss a personal process for selecting books according to illustrations, author, subject matter, reading level, etc. Have each child select a book and then explain the reason(s) for the choice.

Elementary School

Have children talk about programs available on broadcast and cable TV. Have small groups make lists of favorite shows, shows they hate, and shows they are not allowed to watch. Talk about the three lists. Discuss how they make choices about TV shows, considering such things as the characters, the content, and the program's air time. Why are some programs considered off-limits? Discuss how people determine their personal standards and have each child list personal criteria for TV program choices.

Middle School

Have each participant make a list of comic books and magazines under the like and don't like headings. As a group, compare and contrast lists. Discuss how they make choices about the comic books they like, considering such things as the covers, content, and characters. Discuss and list comic books, books, or magazines they are not allowed to read and the reasons. Have each participant make a personal set of criteria for print materials appropriate for middle schoolers. Discuss the criteria.

High School

Have the participants discuss popular music lyrics. Is all popular music the same? Are there specific artists, songs, or styles of music that they consider unacceptable? Discuss whether tapes and CDs should have warning labels. Discuss whether some lyrics should be outlawed such as those promoting sadism, racism, the overthrow of the government, pornography, etc. Have them reflect in journal entries about personal criteria for selecting popular music.

36. EVALUATE "SOUND BITES"

Today TV reporters routinely cut an official's remarks into 10- and 15-second sound bites, then weave these into their own narration. It is the journalist, not the official, who speaks to the news audience.

Daniel Hallin, "We Keep America on Top of the World",
as quoted in *Media & Values*, Spring, 1990

CONCEPT:

Sound bites are quotes taken from a larger text. Because a sound bite is a selected short clip, the quote is someone's judgment about its relevance and worth. Selecting a representative sentence or two from a text is a difficult task and can influence the perceptions and reactions of the viewer, listener, or reader regarding the purpose or meaning of the original text. A quote taken out of its context can be used to deliberately slant an argument or a news presentation.

ACTIVITIES:

Preschool - 1st Grade

Read aloud a picture book that contains a lot of dialog. Choose and read one short statement and ask if this sentence represents everything they know about the character. Discuss a few examples from the book. Why is it unfair to hear just one statement and not the whole conversation? Discuss possible problems.

Elementary School

Have members of the group write summaries of their feelings about an issue such as saving the whales. Then read aloud just one selected sentence from each student's summary. Discuss whether this would be a fair representation of each student's entire viewpoint. Select and read another sentence and discuss this sound bite. Talk about the risks of using quotations without knowing the correct context.

Middle School

Ask participants to read the text of a speech of a famous historical figure, such as John F. Kennedy or Eleanor Roosevelt. Introduce the concept "sound bite." Have each person select a sentence or two that best summarizes the speech. Have each participant read the sound bite aloud out of context. Were different sentences chosen or did all of the participants select the same one? Discuss the subjective judgment involved in sound bite selection and the problems that may occur in using them.

High School

Introduce the concept of sound bites. Have participants watch for news reports that use sound bites. Get a print copy of the speech or other text from which a sound bite was taken and have participants read and discuss the entire copy. Was the sound bite a fair representation? Discuss how sound bites could be used both favorably and unfavorably. Have them select sound bites from famous historical speeches and share them with the group.

37. IDENTIFY JINGLES, SLOGANS, AND ICONS

Our major obligation is not to mistake slogans for solutions.
Edward R. Morrow

CONCEPT:

Jingles and slogans are short catchy phrases created to stick in the minds of consumers. Advertisers use jingles and slogans to link specific ideas or emotional statements to products. "Just Do It!," the well-known slogan that was part of their successful advertising campaign, helped move Nike from the #2 athletic shoe to #1. Icons are representative images that are used to intentionally remind consumers of specific companies or products. The Keebler Elves, for instance, are used in Keebler's TV commercials, packaging, and print ads to reinforce audience recognition of the Keebler products.

ACTIVITIES:

Preschool - 1st Grade

Create an icon board, placing familiar icons of products and companies on posterboard or a bulletin board. An example is the toucan from Fruit Loops cereal. Have children recall what product each image represents. Discuss the purpose of using icons such as Mickey Mouse to represent all products from the Disney Company. Have children start collecting icons for the bulletin board. Discuss each icon and the corresponding product or company.

Elementary School

Create a jingle quiz for children using jingles they would recognize from TV commercials such as the Frosted Flakes jingle, "They're grrrrrrrrrrrrreat!" See how many of them the children know. Discuss reasons that jingles are used in ads. Have the group develop a definition of jingle. Have a contest to create a jingle or slogan for the group. Have judges select the best one and use it in future newsletters or other print materials.

Middle School

Discuss jingles. Have the group members list jingles and pair them with products or companies. Have them analyze the jingles and select the best one. Invite a professional from the advertising industry to visit the group and discuss the power of words when used as jingles or slogans. Have participants create a short and effective jingle or slogan for their school, group, or organization. Use it on stationary or T-shirts.

High School

Study and discuss icons. Ask participants to collect icons and display them on a bulletin board. Analyze the icons and vote for the most effective one. Have each person research and display icons from history and other world cultures, as well as current ones. Have a contest to create an icon to represent the group. Have judges select the best one and have the group use it on all print materials.

Review
Reflect
React!

38. INTERPRET ADVERTISING MESSAGES

The average child sees 20,000 TV commercials every year.
"Facts About Television," *TV-Free America*

CONCEPT:

Advertising is ubiquitous! Media messages that implore us to buy, think, or behave in specific ways are literally everywhere. Consumers must analyze and evaluate all messages - the words and the images - and become more aware of the techniques and purposes of advertising. Advertisements draw us in, stimulate and entertain us, and pressure us to act - purchase, vote, travel, etc. Advertising agencies hire psychologists to help them better understand the audience and employ market researchers to ensure their ads are appealing. Advertising works! Increasing our knowledge and critical thinking skills can offset the power of advertising.

ACTIVITIES:

Preschool - 1st Grade

What is advertising? Why do we see so many ads? Discuss favorite TV commercials. Why are they their favorites? Show videotaped "kidvid" commercials and discuss their appeal. Ask the children if they ever wanted something that was advertised on TV and then, after getting it, were disappointed. Discuss how ads make us want products.

Elementary School

Have children brainstorm a brand new product. Their task is to get people to want this product so they can sell many of them and get rich. How will they tell people about this new product? Discuss the many forms of advertising and predict which ones would work the best for this product. Have them create either print ads or 30-second TV commercials. Analyze which of the ads would be best at encouraging people to buy the product. Have the children discuss reasons for their choices.

Middle School

Ask the participants to list all the places they see advertising. Discuss some unusual places they've seen ads. Why are some ads better in print and others better on TV or radio? Discuss the clothing they are wearing and reasons for their choices. Does advertising work? Invite an advertising professional to the group to discuss the power of advertising. Invite parents and community members to this session. Write journal entries on this topic.

High School

Discuss the power of advertising. Research the history of advertising. Create a questionnaire about the advisability and effectiveness of advertising in schools and distribute it to teachers, parents, administrators, and community leaders. Analyze the results. Discuss hidden forms of advertising in schools. Have participants write letters to the school board sharing the findings and their opinions.

REVIEW
REFLECT
REACT

39. ANALYZE ALCOHOL PRODUCT ADS

It doesn't get any better than this!
slogan for Old Milwaukee Beer

CONCEPT:

Ads that portray the use of alcohol as the catalyst for fun and a required part of the social scene misrepresent reality. It is imperative that people, especially youth, who are exposed to these messages make decisions about alcohol use based on facts, not just on the persuasive tactics of creative advertising agencies. Activities that raise awareness and encourage analysis of alcohol ads are key components of the media literacy process.

ACTIVITIES:

Preschool - 1st Grade

Talk about alcohol products with the children. Invite their parents to the next session and have a group discussion on alcohol use and misuse. Show a few print alcohol ads and discuss "What's wrong with this picture?" Ask parents to continue this discussion in their homes at appropriate times.

Elementary School

Have children discuss alcohol products, listing as many different types as they can. Use construction paper to mount a few selected magazine ads and display them for the children. Discuss the people and settings in these ads. How do the people look? Are they healthy? Are they having fun? Ask the children to do research about the dangers of alcohol, or read aloud an article about the dangers. Discuss whether these ads are misleading. Have the children create new alcohol product ads that include more realistic images and messages.

Middle School

Distribute magazine ads for various alcohol products and discuss their images. Have small groups select alcohol ads and create montages of the images of people in these ads. Research facts about alcohol dangers and discuss whether the images in the ads are misleading. Have the groups create headings or titles for their montages, such as "Don't be fooled by these folks!" Discuss their montages and generalizations that can be made about them. Have the group members reflect in their journals about the alcohol ads.

High School

Have the participants research current use of alcohol products and statistics such as alcohol-related car accidents. Have them watch for, and keep a record of, alcohol product ads over a one-week period, looking at magazine ads, TV commercials, billboards, sporting events, store ads, etc. Discuss the location, audience, content, and impact of this advertising. Have them write letters to the editor of a local newspaper, expressing their concerns.

REVIEW
REFLECT
REACT

40. ANALYZE TOBACCO ADS

From television ads we know that everyone in America smokes.
Georgina Becci, age 13, Buenos Aires, Argentina
"America's New Merchants of Death," *Reader's Digest,*
April, 1993

CONCEPT:

Tobacco advertising has proved to be an important factor in determining whether teens and pre-teens will start smoking or chewing tobacco products. Tobacco use is on the rise, and today's youth must be prepared for a growing onslaught of advertising messages that attempt to counteract existing health education in the homes, schools, and communities. Knowledge of the health dangers of tobacco is not enough. Media literacy training is essential to diminish the persuasive power of tobacco advertising.

ACTIVITIES:

Preschool - 1st Grade

Talk about smoking. Have the children ask their parents about smoking and the dangers of tobacco. Discuss what they learned in their discussions. Show a few cigarette ads and discuss whether the products look appealing or frightening. Why do the ads make cigarettes and smoking look so appealing? Discuss possible reasons, such as "to make children want to smoke when they get older."

Elementary School

Have the children collect magazine ads for tobacco products over a two-week period. Have them sort the ads into various categories, such as by the age or gender of the person portrayed or by the actual product brand. Discuss the dangers of tobacco use. Have each child learn about what happens in the human body when tobacco products are used. Analyze the ads for facts about these dangers. What conclusions can they draw?

Middle School

Discuss the use of chewing tobacco. Have the participants find ads for these products and bring them to the group meeting. Have them do research about the dangers of chewing tobacco. Discuss whether sports figures, such as baseball players, should be allowed to chew tobacco while they play. Have each person write a letter to a favorite baseball player or team about the use of chewing tobacco.

High School

Have the participants do research to determine whether tobacco is a drug. Present and discuss the reports. Track tobacco advertising at stores, at sporting events, in magazines, on billboards, etc. over a two-week period. Discuss their observations. Have them research why tobacco ads were removed from TV. How do advertisers offset the known dangers of tobacco use? What tricks or tactics do they employ? Lead the group members in a discussion of actions they can take regarding the bombardment of youth with tobacco messages by the mass media. Have each small group select one action and complete it. Report back to the whole group.

41. QUESTION HISTORICAL ACCURACY

We Americans are the best informed people on earth as to the events of the last twenty-four hours; we are not the best informed as to the events of the last sixty centuries.

Will and Ariel Durant

CONCEPT:

For the sake of entertainment or "artistic license," facts regarding historical events, people, or motives are changed. This is done intentionally to create a more dramatic scene or make a political statement, or it is simply due to a lack of information. Since millions of viewers, listeners, or readers may be affected by the distortion of history, it is important to fully understand that the purpose of the entertainment industry is to make money. Entertainment media should not be considered as reliable sources of historical information, but merely regarded as "historical fiction."

ACTIVITIES:

Preschool - 1st Grade

Discuss the Pocahontas cartoon character in the Disney movie. Read a story to the group about the real Pocahontas. Compare and contrast the two depictions. Does anyone know what Pocahontas really looked like? Why not? Have the children discuss other famous people from history, such as Christopher Columbus, and whether we really know what they looked or acted like.

Elementary School

Make a list of historical characters the group members have seen portrayed in movies. Each child is to select one and compile a list of facts about that person's real life actions, motives, appearance, etc. Then compare/contrast the findings with the movie portrayals. Discuss the findings.

Middle School

Have the group research a historical character, such as Molly Brown, who has been depicted in a movie. Show the group a photo or drawing of the person. Watch the movie about that historical person, such as "The Unsinkable Molly Brown." Compare and contrast the actual person with the movie character. What conclusions might participants draw from this?

High School

Have group members create a list of movies that have supposedly been based on true events. Discuss whether all of the facts in the movies were accurate. How can they find out? Have small groups of participants work together to:
- Select a movie with a historical setting;
- Watch the movie, making a list of questions;
- Find the correct answers in reference sources to verify or refute the movie's accuracy.

Discuss the findings. What are their conclusions regarding historical accuracy in movies?

42. JUDGE THE RELIABILITY OF THE SOURCE

Skepticism is a hedge against vulnerability.
Charles Thomas Samuels

CONCEPT:

Not all information sources are equal. It is necessary to create standards of acceptability in order to determine which sources to believe. For example, is a billboard message as reliable a source as a CNN news report? Children and teenagers need assistance to examine the onslaught of media messages and to create a personal hierarchy of reliability standards. With the popularity of the Internet and the advent of 500-channel TV, this issue becomes even more important. Critical thinkers do not treat all messages as fact, but possess the discernment to give more credence to some than to others.

ACTIVITIES:

Preschool - 1st Grade

Show pictures of various information sources, such as a TV, book, newspaper, radio, etc. Ask children to talk about what they can learn from each one. Discuss several communication sources and their differences.

Elementary School

Ask children how they learn about the world around them. Make a list of their answers. Are some of the sources better for certain information? For example, if they want to find out the weather forecast for tomorrow, would an encyclopedia be the best source? Have small groups list sources and the best information to get from each. Compare and discuss their answers. Make one composite list and distribute it to the children.

Middle School

Discuss the Internet and how it may affect the participants' lives. How reliable is the information that is available on the Internet? How do the group members know what is true? Have them spend time accessing information via the Internet. Discuss their findings. Have them write a journal entry, "Are all information sources equal?"

High School

Have each group member select a topic to research. Have each person list appropriate sources for the research. Discuss whether all sources are reliable. For example, is a tabloid newspaper a dependable source? Explain. Discuss the basis on which they make their decisions about the reliability of a source. Have the participants research their topics and determine which sources were the most reliable. Explain reasons for rejecting some sources as unreliable. Share the findings and develop a general hierarchy of reliability of sources.

REVIEW
REFLECT
REACT

43. RECOGNIZE DECEPTIVE MARKETING

Advertising may be described as the science of arresting the human intelligence long enough to get money from it.

Stephen Leacock

CONCEPT:

Advertising strategies can transcend mere exaggeration and be outright unethical or untruthful. To recognize the gimmicks and hook lines of marketing ploys requires knowledge, skill, and discernment. Snake oil sales tactics are enticing, and the expression, "buyer beware!" is an important warning for all consumers to heed. New telemarketing techniques, frenetic lifestyles, and access to people's private data files increase the potential for consumers to be fleeced. Intricate scams on the Internet prey on naive people. Advertising enticements such as "$1 over sticker price" or "Lose 30 pounds in 30 days for $30" appeal to consumers who are hoping to get a bargain. Raising the awareness of young people is necessary in order to help them be more discerning.

ACTIVITIES:

Preschool - 1st Grade

Have children define and give examples of opinions, exaggerations, and lies. Discuss advertising messages for products the children know. Have the children discuss and label each message as either an opinion, an exaggeration, or a lie. Have the children change the messages into extreme exaggerations or outright lies and discuss the differences they notice.

Elementary School

Distribute newspapers to the children. Discuss advertising strategies that are used to hook consumers: bold print, give-aways, fine print, "free," etc. Have the children search through the newspapers to collect examples of enticements used in ads. Discuss which ones seem too good to be true. Have each child interview an adult about being ripped off, to include some examples.

Middle School

Have the group members discuss advertising strategies that are used to entice consumers. Discuss ways to recognize misleading offers. Discuss the importance of never disclosing personal information over the phone or via the Internet. Have them spend time looking for examples of incredible offers or possible scams on the Internet. Discuss their findings. Have them write in their journals about enticements that seemed too good to be true.

High School

Discuss examples of dishonest advertising strategies and deceptive marketing ploys. Have the participants research the topic of consumer fraud and report their findings to the group. Have them read recent articles about cases of defrauding the elderly. Locate information about helpful organizations or fraud protection information available for senior citizens. Have participants create a brochure or flyer listing fraud awareness information, and distribute them to local senior citizen groups. Have them write journal entries about deceptive advertising strategies.

Review Reflect React

44. ANALYZE MUSIC LYRICS

It [rock music] remains one of the most important and most over-looked social forces in mass communication.

Mediamerica

CONCEPT:

Music is a powerful and meaningful way to communicate. The form and content of music, especially popular music, lets us know that music is more than just a relaxing experience. It can produce emotional reactions, camaraderie, and even social change. Adding lyrics to music sends messages that can entertain, motivate, arouse, and even irritate listeners. Media literacy mandates that the messages contained in the lyrics be accurately interpreted to assess the impact of popular music.

ACTIVITIES:

Preschool - 1st Grade

> Select a new song for the children to learn. First teach them the words and then repeat the melody until they know the new song. Have the children listen to the music without words. Then have them sing the newly learned words to a melody they already know. Did using a different tune alter the lyrics or their reactions?

Elementary School

> Have the group listen on different occasions to various styles of music, such as rock, rap, blues, and classical. Play a tape of a song that is already familiar to them. Have the children read and analyze the lyrics without the music. What message is the song sending? Listen to other songs and analyze their lyrics. Discuss the importance of lyrics.

Middle School

> Select a song such as "The Star Spangled Banner," that has a story, and distribute a copy of the words to each person. Before hearing the melody, have the group read and analyze the lyrics for form, rhythm, expression, purpose, etc. Have the group members perform a choral reading of the words before an audience. Finally, have them listen to a tape of the song - the lyrics with the melody - and discuss what effects the melody had on the words.

High School

> Have each group member choose one appropriate song, write down and analyze the lyrics without the melody. Are the words a poem? Is the meaning clear without the music? Does the melody add to or detract from the message of the lyrics? Then have each person create new lyrics for the same melody. Compare and contrast the old and new lyrics. Discuss whether lyrics of popular music provide social commentary. Discuss current popular songs and analyze the lyrics.

Review
Reflect
React

45. REFLECT ON THE NEED TO READ

There is more treasure in books than in all the pirates' loot on Treasure Island...and best of all, you can enjoy these riches every day of your life.

Walt Disney

CONCEPT:

Why read? The instant access to information through 24-hour-a-day newscasts on radio and TV minimizes the felt need to read. Some legitimate reasons to read persist, however, including the diverse range of subject matter in print media, in-depth coverage, historical perspective, commentary, and reference options. Perhaps most significant among the reasons, though, is that reading enables young people to develop vocabulary, understand writing styles, appreciate different perspectives, and experience vicarious adventures. Reading is as relevant today as it ever was.

ACTIVITIES:

Preschool - 1st Grade

Plan a quiet reading time every day. Discuss why books are part of our lives. Have children share their favorite books and why some appeal to them more than others. Talk about the two categories of books (fiction and nonfiction) and why both are important. Read aloud every day and allow children to discuss the stories.

Elementary School

Read aloud often from a variety of books and print materials. Discuss ways in which books are different from movies, TV, and video games. Compare and contrast the experience of reading a book with the viewing of the electronic version, such as a movie, based on the same story. Have children read and compare different genre such as historical fiction, fantasy, poetry, adventure, nonfiction, etc. Have them keep a personal record of books and magazines read. After a period of time, have each person reflect on what they have read. Discuss why everyone needs to read.

Middle School

Discuss favorite books. Have participants spend time each day reading books of their choice. Have group members make a composite list of relevant reasons to read. Have them work in small groups to create a print ad about the importance of reading. Have the ad printed in a local newspaper or posted in the local library or school. Have them reflect in their journals on the necessity to read, especially in today's electronic media-saturated society.

High School

Have participants select a topic and read a wide variety of books, magazines, Internet articles, etc. on that topic. Then invite one or more local experts to discuss that topic with the group. Discuss how reading expanded their knowledge of the topic so they had the necessary background for the discussion. Have them reflect in their journals on the subject, "Why Read?"

46. RELATE DEMOCRACY TO MEDIA LITERACY

Democracy depends on information circulating freely in society.
Katherine Graham, former publisher of the *Washington Post*

CONCEPT:

Democracy is defined by *Webster's New Collegiate Dictionary* as "a government by the people." Processing and reflecting on information, images, and messages from the print and electronic media is an essential part of being a citizen in a democracy. The electoral process includes extensive advertising campaigns, polls, and political strategizing, all of which influence public opinion and ultimately the election results. Media literacy skills are also democracy skills. Citizens must become critical thinkers about all aspects of the political system. This includes being actively involved in the electoral process and providing feedback to elected government officials.

ACTIVITIES:

Preschool - 1st Grade

Discuss what voting means. Have the group practice this concept whenever possible, such as voting for favorite snacks, favorite pictures in a book, or favorite games to play. Explain that each child can vote for one favorite per category. Use this process to decide on activities or food choices, for example, to help the children understand that the majority rules.

Elementary School

Read aloud the book, *The Voice of the People: American Democracy in Action*, by Maestro, and discuss the concepts listed. Discuss how citizens get their information about political candidates, issues, and current events. Have group members research what is meant by a free press. Discuss the importance of a free press.

Middle School

Have the participants research the components of a democracy. Discuss why free speech is such an important concept in a democracy. Research examples of free speech issues in U.S. history. Discuss the numerous ways citizens can express themselves in our society. Have each participant create an acrostic for the word democracy, such as D is for the Democratic Party, E is for equality, etc.

High School

Have teenagers research the role of journalism in U.S. history, dating back to pre-Revolutionary war days. Discuss the role of the mass media in a democratic society vs. their role in a dictatorship. Invite an elected official to the group to answer questions about political campaigning. Have participants reflect in their journals about the role of the mass media in the political process.

RESOURCES:

"What is a Democracy?" (grades 2-6), video and instructional materials from the series, "MY AMERICA: Building a Democracy," New Castle Communications, Inc. (see Additional Resources section)

Review
Reflect
React!

47. EXAMINE THE ROLE OF THE INDIVIDUAL IN A DEMOCRACY

I am only one, but I am still one. I cannot do everything, but I can do something; and because I cannot do everything I will not refuse to do the something that I can do.

Edward Everett Hale

CONCEPT:

One person can alter the ideas, behavior, or philosophy of a group. In the history of nations, a succession of individuals have been responsible for significant changes in political or social direction. Mass media messages rarely focus on how one individual can shape destiny. It is important that the youth do not become defeated by an impersonal and highly mediated world. Instead, they need to learn that one person can still make a difference!

ACTIVITIES:

Preschool - 1st Grade

Discuss how one child can affect the group, either positively or negatively. Have the children give examples of this concept. Read aloud a picture book, such as *The Emperor's New Clothes*, that illustrates how one individual made a difference in the lives of others. Discuss the main character, the story, and, most important, the changes that one person caused.

Elementary School

Discuss how a democratic society works. Why is it important to vote? Can one person make a difference? Discuss familiar situations where one person made a difference in the lives of others. Name characters in movies where the ideas, behavior, or attitude of one individual affected others. Have the children bring in newspaper stories where one person made a difference. Discuss each situation.

Middle School

Discuss how the mass media are involved in the political process today. Have the participants do research about famous Americans, such as Thomas Jefferson and Martin Luther King, who have shaped our democratic process. Have group members write letters to these famous historical figures, explaining how today's mass media affect the democratic system in the United States. Have the letters published in the school or local newspaper.

High School

How do the people in a democracy find out about political candidates and issues? Discuss the role of the mass media in a democracy. List some factors that influence voters. Have the participants "surf the net" to find information about our political system. Discuss the role of the Internet in the political process. Discuss whether this communication medium will alter the democratic system by facilitating the input of citizens' opinions. Conduct an essay contest on the topic, "Can one person (or one vote) still make a difference?" Have them share and discuss their writings. Let them select the best one to submit to a newspaper or magazine or to place on the Internet.

Review
Reflect React

48. RECOGNIZE THE POSITIVE ROLE OF THE MASS MEDIA

The cable television industry provides "schools with free basic cable service and more than 525 hours of commercial-free educational programming each month."
Cable in the Classroom, July/August, 1996

CONCEPT:

The power of the mass media cannot be overstated. Print and electronic media influence the lives of most people. The mass media can directly contribute to the welfare of an individual, a family, a community, or an organization by disseminating information and generating concern. TV programs, newspaper ads, PSAs, flyers, radio announcements, and editorials can cause positive results such as finding missing children, raising money, fostering support for victims, or focusing a community. The investigative function of the media is well known. Exposés can bring truth to light, dishonest people to justice, and corporations to their knees. The media can deliver good news about outstanding citizens, educational institutions, non-profit organizations, and community efforts. By examining the range of media responsibilities, individuals will have a balanced view of the role of the mass media.

ACTIVITIES:

Preschool - 1st Grade

Have children discuss some good things they learned from TV such as how to call 911, safety practices, health habits, etc. How can these help in their daily lives? Discuss some examples of how these have helped a friend or family member.

Elementary School

Talk about recent news stories that show the positive power of the mass media. This might be a story of people helping victims of a disaster, or a missing person report that ended happily. Talk about TV programs like "Rescue 911" or "America's Most Wanted" and how these shows can help people. List ways the print and electronic media positively serve society.

Middle School

Have the group create a bulletin board or poster that is called "Good Work!" For the display have the youth find examples of positive uses of the print media, such as a PSA about the dangers of drug use, news stories about communities working together, successful school stories, positive editorials, or ads of upcoming free cultural events. Have participants write a journal entry, "The Positive Power of the Press."

High School

Review
Reflect
React

Divide the participants into two groups. One group will tally print, radio, and TV PSAs over a 2-week period. Have them contact the local media to find out specific requirements regarding PSAs. The other group will analyze the nightly TV news programs and note any stories that are evidence of the positive role of the media such as helping to find a lost child or a food drive for the homeless. Bring the two groups together to discuss the positive role of the media.

49. MAKE MEDIA MESSAGES

Tell me and I remember. Involve me and I understand.

Chinese proverb

CONCEPT:

Learning the active steps involved in producing media messages reinforces media literacy concepts. Some of the steps are to determine the desired message, the targeted audience, the selected medium, the content (both images and text), the precise production requirements, and the anticipated impact of the message. At the outset of any project involving the making of media, it is critical that analysis and evaluation of existing media become part of the procedure. By actually creating a final product, we can begin to learn about the potential power of the media and the responsibility of media makers.

ACTIVITIES:

Preschool - 1st Grade

Discuss the concept that each human being is unique and important. Have each child create a personal poster with both picture and name. On the top of each poster, write, "Please handle with care. I'm important!" Display the posters in areas where lots of people will see them. Discuss how people might react to the posters.

Elementary School

Have the children discuss a topic for a mural to be created as a group project. Consider content, location, potential audience, and required materials. Have the group members first create a rough draft that is the actual size of the proposed mural. Discuss the impact and the point-of-view of the draft. Make necessary changes. Then create the final product and arrange for some press coverage of this project.

Middle School

Discuss messages that are seen on clothing items, such as T-shirts, hats, jackets, etc. Have each participant create an important non-commercial message that could be placed on an item of clothing. Discuss each message with other participants and modify as needed. Have each participant bring to the next meeting an item of clothing for the message. Provide the materials needed for the project, such as cloth paints or crayons. Have them place the message on their clothing. Discuss the impact of the final products, including the potential audience for the messages.

High School

Consider topics for a PSA for television. Have small groups design scripts, setting, characters, point of view, props, etc. for their 30-second spots. Videotape the final products. View and discuss each one and analyze the message and its potential impact. Have the group select the most effective PSA. Contact the local TV stations to see if any will air the spots. In addition, air the spots on a closed-circuit system at a school or on a community-access TV channel.

RESOURCES:

Using the Media, activity book for grades 4-8, Carson-Dellosa Publishing Co., Inc. (see Additional Resources section)

REVIEW
REFLECT
REACT

50. THINK FOR YOURSELF

*There are two ways to slide easily through life; to believe every-
thing or to doubt everything. Both ways save us from thinking.*
Alfred Korzybski

CONCEPT:

Regardless of the vast number of messages that bombard people everyday, it is up to each individual to sort through them, determine which ones are reliable, and discount the rest. The mass
media must never assume that the citizens are merely pawns in a mediated chess game. Everyone
must take the responsibility of becoming a critical thinker, even though it is easier to accept or
reject others' ideas. The consequences of dismissing messages as "just advertising," "just news,"
or "just entertainment" are too great. Media literate citizens recognize that they must become
engaged in the process of critical thinking - reviewing, reflecting, reacting - everyday.

ACTIVITIES:

Preschool - 1st Grade

Select some activities that are open ended and that do not have specific right answers.
For example, place an unusual object on the table and ask children to decide what it is.
Allow them to use their imaginations to formulate answers, such as homework machine.
Be non-judgmental in reacting to their answers. Plan these activities often and encourage
children to think for themselves.

Elementary School

Discuss the importance of critical thinking. Have a poster contest with the theme, "Think
for Yourself!" Have the children design posters that will encourage others to review,
reflect, and react to media messages. Invite parents to be judges and select a few winners. Notify the local newspaper of the contest and the winning posters. Display the
posters in a community setting such as the local library, school, or post office.

Middle School

Discuss how thinking is often shaped by the anticipated reactions of others. Discuss how
it is harder to think independently than to accept the thoughts of others. Have the participants share examples of times they thought for themselves. Have small groups brainstorm
ideas for short skits for young audiences, based on the theme, "Think for Yourself!" Have
the groups write scripts, assign roles, get props and costumes, and then perform their skits
for young children. Videotape the skits and have the group discuss their effectiveness.

High School

Explain that each individual must sort through all the messages received and then "think
for yourself." Discuss the importance of the 3Rs - review, reflect, and react. Have the participants do the necessary research and create a script for a talk show, inviting "guests" -
historical, political, or fictional folks with appropriate costumes - to explain how they
thought for themselves, rather than merely accepting the thinking of others. Videotape
the talk show and air it on a school or community access channel.

GLOSSARY

AIR TIME is the time allocated to a particular program, announcement, or commercial. It is a concept used in broadcasting. Air time is sold by the advertising departments.

CUTS refers to splices or edits. When viewers become aware of the frequency of edits in a 30-second TV commercial, for instance, they realize that this is a technique intentionally designed to hold their attention.

DE-CONSTRUCTING means analyzing all the components, such as the color, background, lighting, people and clothing in a media presentation. Advertisements and other media messages are constructed to create audience interest.

ENVIRONMENTAL PRINT is education jargon for print materials that are found in homes and communities. The print environment includes messages, such as signs, cereal boxes, bumper stickers, clothing, and billboards, that children read in their everyday surroundings.

GATEKEEPER is the term for a media industry decision maker, such as a producer, editor, or news director. This individual impacts the standards for content, and is thus responsible for selecting the information that reaches the masses.

GENRE is defined by *Webster's New Collegiate Dictionary* as "a category of artistic, musical, or literary composition characterized by a particular style, form, or content." Television programming can be labeled by specific genres, such as talk shows, sitcoms, news programs, commercials, etc.

HOME PAGE is a page of information that can be accessed via the Internet. It can be text, images, or a combination of both, and can be developed for commercial purposes or individual use.

INFOTAINMENT is a new term for the blend of information and entertainment into a hybrid format such as news magazine TV programs.

KIDVID refers to television programming aimed specifically at children. Kidvid commercials are ads meant to be aired on Saturday morning or during other children's programming blocks.

JOLTS are incidents of humor, sexual innuendo, fast-paced action, or violence that grab the TV viewers' attention. Jolts are often intentionally placed in scenes that may otherwise cause viewers to change channels (especially since the advent of the remote control device). TV commercials are filled with jolts to ensure that viewers will stay tuned.

MASS MEDIA are methods of communication, such as the radio, television, or newspapers that use technology to reach many people.

MEDIA LITERACY refers to the skills and knowledge needed to question, analyze, interpret, and evaluate messages of the mass media. Other terms commonly used are "media education" and "media studies."

MORPHING is a computer technique that allows one image to be carefully superimposed onto another so that the change is instantaneous to viewers. This has recently become a popular strategy to hold the viewer's attention in music videos and TV commercials.

POV is the abbreviation for "point of view." The POV is the viewpoint of the author, creator, director, character, or even the camera. The POV can affect the impact of the message.

PSA is the abbreviation for "Public Service Announcement." A PSA is aired or printed at no cost to its sponsor.

REALITY DRAMA is a term for a television program based on real-life situations but that uses actors in dramatizations. This blurs the line between reality and fantasy.

SITCOM is an abbreviated form of "situation comedy." It is a popular TV show genre. The setting, characters, and their relationships remain constant from week to week, with new plots developing around the same people.

SOUND BITE is a quote taken out of a larger text. For example, when time constraints will not permit a TV news program to air an entire speech, a portion that is considered representative of the whole is chosen to let the viewers hear its essence. Because of the selective nature of a sound bite, this decision can be very influential.

SPOTS are radio and TV advertisements.

TABLOID NEWS originally referred to a newspaper format smaller than the traditional newspapers. Today, this term is used to describe sensationalized news that includes purchased stories and photographs.

VERBAL VIOLENCE is profanity, hate language, and verbal threats. Incidents of verbal violence have increased dramatically in the entertainment media. This violence subset has recently been separated from the more generic study of violence so it can be dealt with more specifically.

ADDITIONAL RESOURCES

BOOKS:

Considine, David M., and Gail E. Haley. *Visual Messages: Integrating Imagery into Instruction.* Englewood: Libraries Unlimited, 1992. A great curriculum guide with activities and background information. It is a must for every school's professional library.

Considine, David M., Gail E. Haley, and Lyn Ellen Lacy. *Imagine That: Developing Critical Thinking and Critical Viewing Through Children's Literature.* Englewood: Libraries Unlimited, 1994. This curriculum guide has engaging activities to teach media literacy through picture books and is an excellent guide for every elementary school.

Duncan, Barry. *Mass Media & Popular Culture.* Toronto: Harcourt Brace Jovanovich, 1988. Aimed at middle school and high school students, this book is a compilation of articles on the mass media's involvement in our culture.

Duncan, Barry, et al. *Mass Media & Popular Culture.* Version 2. Toronto: Harcourt Brace Jovanovich, 1996. An updated version, filled with appropriate readings that serve as informative background and excellent discussion starters for middle school and high school students.

Lloyd-Kolkin, Donna, and Kathleen Tyner. *Media & You: An Elementary Media Literacy Curriculum.* Englewood Cliffs: Educational Technology Publications, 1991. An excellent resource for teachers in elementary schools.

Pipher, Dr. Mary. *Reviving Ophelia.* New York: G. P. Putnam's Sons, 1994. This book is an examination of the influence of the popular culture on middle school-aged girls.

Silverblatt, Art. *Media Literacy: Keys to Interpreting Media Messages.* Westport: Praeger, 1995. A textbook serving as an overview for teachers, it thoroughly explains communications and media literacy concepts.

Winn, Marie. *The Plug-In Drug.* New York: Penguin Books, 1985. This book is a worthwhile look at the role of television in the home.

BOOKLETS/BROCHURES/HAND-OUTS:

"Media Literacy: Introductory Concepts, Resources, and Activities," $5. Contact: New Mexico Media Literacy Project (NMMLP); 6400 Wyoming NE; Albuquerque, NM 87109; 505-828-3264; e-mail: mccannon@aa.edu; URL: http://www.aa.edu/www.html.

"Media Literacy: Training Tips for the Home," $1 each; "Media Literacy: Training Tips for the Classroom," $1 each. Contact: PRIIME TIIME Today; P. O. Box 2829; Littleton, CO 80161; 303-770-3239.

"Media Violence: 10 Tips for Parents," free. Contact: Turn Off the Violence; P. O. Box 27558; Minneapolis, MN 55427.

"Media Violence and Children," $.50 each. Contact: Association for the Education of Young Children; 1509 16th Street, NW; Washington, DC 20036-1426; 800-424-2460.

MAGAZINES:

"*Zillions*," grades 4-8. This Consumer Reports magazine is informational and causes young people to think about merchandising techniques and products that are available.. Contact: Zillions; Box 2878; Boulder, CO 80322.

MULTIMEDIA KITS:

"Beyond Blame: Challenging Violence in the Media," grades 4-12, adults. This comprehensive multimedia program includes videotapes, guide, reproducible handouts, background resources, etc. $249.95 for entire kit (Portions can be purchased separately.)

"Selling Addiction," grades 7-12, adults. This is a valuable resource exposing the myths and deceptions of tobacco and alcohol advertising. $99.95.

"TV Alert: A Wake-Up Guide for Television Literacy," grades 7-12, adults This kit has a video and activity guide to cause participants to analyze the TV experience. $79.95.

For the above three titles, contact: The Center for Media Literacy; 4727 Wilshire Blvd., Suite 403 Los Angeles, CA 90010; 800-226-9494 (ask for a free catalog); http://www.earth-link.net/~CML.

"Beyond the Front Page," grades 7-12. This is a series of 10 videos, each 25 minutes, covering the making of the newspaper, behind-the-scenes activities, and writing workshops.

"Don't Stop the Presses - How the Newspaper Works." (video #1), is a useful media literacy resource for teaching about the newspaper. $34.95/program

For the above two titles, contact: GPN; P. O. Box 80669; Lincoln, Nebraska 68501-0669; 800-228-4630.

"Creating Critical TV Viewers," grades 4-12, adults. This kit contains six video segments on one 77-minute videotape plus a comprehensive workbook written by educators at Yale's Family Television Research Center. $59.95. Contact: GPN (see address listed above)

"Scanning Television: Videos for Media Literacy in Class," grades 7-12, adults. This excellent resource contains 4 one-hour videotapes and a detailed teacher's guide. This is a useful compilation of video segments for schools and organizations integrating media literacy into their curriculum. $229. Contact: National Telemedia Council, Inc.; 120 East Wilson Street; Madison, WI 53703; 608-257-7712; e-mail: NTelemedia@aol.com.

"What is a Democracy?," grades 2-6. This kit contains an engaging video and instructional materials from the series, "MY AMERICA: Building a Democracy." $99. Contact: New Castle Communications, Inc.; 229 King Street; Chappaqua, New York 10514; 800-723-1263.

NIE (NEWSPAPER IN EDUCATION) MATERIALS:

"Media Literacy: a two-part guide to create discerning readers of print and images," grades 4-8. This newspaper curriculum guide is a great starting place for those using the newspaper to teach media literacy skills. Contact: NIE Department, Attention: Jill Scott; The Denver Post; 1560 Broadway; Denver, CO 80202 ; 303-820-1335.

"Making Messages: A Family Activity Guide" "Mastering the Message" (the 1996 "Newspaper in Education Week" guide). These are very valuable Newspaper in Education curriculum guides. Contact the NIE Program of the local newspaper.

POSTER:

"Real/Fantasy Violence" Poster, $3.50. This poster has small print, but excellent content. Contact: NEWIST/CESA #7 ; Studio B, IS 1040; University of Wisconsin, Green Bay, WI 54311; 800-633-7445.

PRINT RESOURCES/UNITS AND CURRICULUM GUIDES:

"Citizenship in a Media Age," grades 7-12, adults. This is a media literacy workshop on democracy and the rights and responsibilities of citizens and is an excellent tool for analyzing campaign strategies and news sources. Contact: The Center for Media Literacy (see address listed above under "Multimedia Kits")

"Heroes," grades 4-8 . This is an excellent interdisciplinary unit which concentrates on the characteristics of heroes. $14.95. Contact: Teacher Created Materials, Inc.; P. O. Box 1040; Huntington Beach, CA 92647; 800-662-4321.

"Hooray for Heroes," grades 1-12. This resource is a great compilation of ideas for introducing the concept of heroes into home, scouting, or school settings. $27.50. Contact: Scarecrow Press; 800-462-6420.

"Living in the Image Culture," grades 7-12, adults. Mass media's images influence ideas, values, and our use of time and money. This resource causes youth and adults to examine those images. $32.95. Contact: The Center for Media Literacy (see address listed above under "Kits")

"Using the Media to Teach Reading and Writing Skills," grades 4-8. This is an easy-to-use reproducible activity book for elementary and middle school students. Mark Twain Media, $9.95. Contact: Carson-Dellosa Publishing Co.; P. O. Box 35665; Greensboro, NC 27425-5665; 800-321-0943.

PRINT RESOURCES/ARTICLES:

"Are Music and Movies Killing America's Soul?", *Time*, June 12, 1995.

"Heroes for Today", a monthly feature in *Reader's Digest* .

"Media and Violence, Part One: Making the Connections." "Media and Violence, Part Two: Searching for Solutions" These two magazines serve as excellent resources for classroom or community involvement in media literacy efforts. The two publications contain necessary background information and pose possible solutions regarding media violence in our society. $3.50 each. Contact: The Center for Media Literacy (see address listed above under "Multimedia Kits")

"The Quest for Media Literacy," *Cable in the Classroom* magazine, June, 1996.

"Television and Violence: The Scale of the Problem and Where To Go From Here." *Journal of the American Medical Association*, June 10, 1992.

"To See or Not To See: the childhood TV viewing dilemma." *School Safety* (newsletter, National School Safety Center News Service), April, 1995.

"TV Violence: The issue is politics more than production." *KidScreen*, January, 1996.

"Video Game Violence." *Zillions* , April/May, 1994.

SOFTWARE:

"Violence in the Media," grades 5-12. This interesting resource includes a computer disk, 28 student reference books, teacher's guide, and an activity guide with lesson plans and reproducible worksheets. It contains some thought-provoking activities for use on either Mac or MS-DOS. $149.95 for 1-computer license. Contact: Tom Snyder Productions; 800-342-0236

TELEVISION PROGRAMS:

"CNN Newsroom," grades 6-12. This is a great commercial-free 15-minute news and current events program. 4:30 am, EST, Monday- Friday on the local CNN cable channel.

"C-SPAN," grades 7-12. Watch for age-appropriate programming on political candidates and issues.

VIDEOS:

"Are You What You Watch?," grades 4-8; "It's Only Television," grades 4-8 ; Nick News Special Reports, Nickelodeon Channel, Cable TV. These 30-minute Lucky Duck productions are interesting and appealing programs that can jump-start lively discussions. Contact: Cable in the Classroom Magazine for upcoming repeat telecasts

"Buy Me That: Kid's Survival Guide to TV Advertising," grades 1-6, $49.95; "Buy Me That, Too: Kid's Guide to TV Advertising," grades 4-8, $69.95; "Buy Me That, Three: Kid's Guide to TV Advertising," grades 4-8, $49.95. These excellent 30-minute programs, created by Consumer Reports, have been aired on HBO. $159.95 for the set of three videos. Contact: The Center for Media Literacy (see address listed above under "Multimedia Kits")

"Cartoons Go To War," grades 9-12, adults. This one-hour A & E documentary about the strategy of using cartoons to influence the audience during World War II is an excellent resource for developing analytical viewing skills. Contact: *Cable in the Classroom* magazine for upcoming telecasts or call A & E.

"Does TV Kill?," grades 9-12, adults. This 90-minute documentary looks at television violence and its impact on our culture. It includes a 15-minute discussion, facilitated by Bill Moyers, with a panel of experts. $69.95 Contact: PBS Video; Public Broadcasting Service; 1320 Braddock Place; Alexandria, VA 22314-1698; 800-344-3337. To obtain classroom activities related to this program: Contact: Frontline; Attention: Diane Hebert; 125 Western Ave.; Boston, MA 02134; 617-783-3500.

"Dreamworlds II," grades 9-12, adults (preview first!) This 1-hour video raises timely questions and analyzes the impact of images seen on MTV videos. This video contains some graphic scenes. $75 for individuals, $125 for non-profit. Contact: Media Education Foundation; 26 Center Street; Northampton, MA 01060; 413-586-4170; URL: http://www.ipc.apc.org/mes.

"Getting the Message Across," grades 9-12, adults. This is a 30-minute video on how to make videos that emphasizes effective communication, narrative, and successful story-telling. $100 non-profit, $60 individual. Contact: Media Education Foundation (see address above)

"The Image Makers"; "The 30-Second President"; Part of the "A Walk through the 20th Century with Bill Moyers" Video Series, the two programs are particularly useful with grades 9-12 and college level students. $69.95 each. Contact: PBS Video (see address listed above)

"The Killing Screens: Media and the Culture of Violence," grades 9-12, adults. This 37-minute video discusses violent messages in the media. $75 individual, $125 non-profit. Contact: Media Education Foundation (see address above)

"Kids Killing Kids" & "Kids Saving Kids", grades 7-12. This video shows dramatizations of four stories, telling each story two ways: with guns and without guns. This is followed by a documentary featuring alternatives to violence. Contact: The nearest Blockbuster Video Store.

"Making Grimm Movies," grades 4-12. This is an excellent media literacy series with a behind-the-scenes look at the making of movies. All 3 parts are on one video, and a 48 page handbook, "The Guide to Making Grimm Movies," is available. $29.95 video, $5 guide. Contact: Davenport Films; 11324 Pearlstone Lane; Delaplane, Virginia 20144-1722; 540-592-3701; URL: http://www.oz.net/~davfilms.

"Media Mayhem: More Than Make Believe," grades 7-12. This is a 30-minute video with teacher's guide that serves as a great discussion starter. $195 ($50 rental) Contact: NEWIST/CESA #7 (See address listed under "Posters")

"On Television: Teach the Children," grades 9-12, adults. This 1-hour video serves as an overview on the influence of TV on children. It includes a 16 page Parent/Teacher Guide and transcript. Available at a special price for PTAs: $29.95. Contact: California Newsreel; 149 Ninth Street; San Francisco, CA 94103; 415-621-6196.

"Pack of Lies: The Advertising of Tobacco," grades 9-12, adults. This 35-minute video is an exposé of advertising strategies of the tobacco industry. $225. Contact: Media Education Foundation (see address above)

"The Power of Newsprint," grades 7-12, adults. This 38-minute video plus the tabloid-style newspapers are excellent teaching tools to analyze advertising techniques. $79. Contact: Lynne Meena & Co.; 85 Fourth Avenue; New York, NY 10003; 212-989-4590.

"Prevent Violence with Groark" video series, grades K-5. This series has five 30-minute videos, each with a teacher's guide. $69.95 each, or $299.50 for set of 5. Contact: GPN; P. O. Box 80669; Lincoln, Nebraska 68501-0669; 800-228-4630.

"Slim Hopes: Advertising and the Obsession with Thinness," grades 9-12, adults. This 30-minute video deals with advertising's messages to females. $215. Contact: Media Education Foundation (see address above)

"Tuning in to Media," grades 7-12, adults. This 30-minute video examines how media messages are constructed. It serves as an excellent introduction to media literacy. $39.95. Contact: GPN (see address listed above)

"What Can We Do About Violence?," grades 9-12, college, adults. This four-part Bill Moyers special is an excellent resource. (4 hours) The "Violence in the Media" segment is a useful overview about the impact of media violence. $89.95 per part. Contact: Films For the Humanities. 800-257-5126

ORGANIZATIONS:

- Association for Media Literacy, 40 McArthur Street, Weston, Ontario, Canada M9P 3M7; 416-394-6992; e-mail: loon@maple.net
- Center for Media Education, 1511 K Street NW, Suite 518, Washington, D.C. 20005; 202-628-2620; info@cme.org; URL: http://www.cme.org/cme
- The Center for Media Literacy, 4727 Wilshire Blvd., Suite 403, Los Angeles, CA 90010; 800-226-9494; URL: http://www.earthlink.net/~CML
- Citizens for Media Literacy, 34 Wall Street, Suite 407, Asheville, NC 28801; 704-255-018; fax 704-254-2286; e-mail: wallyb@main.nc.us
- Media Alert!, 7473 West Laurel Ave., Littleton, CO 80123; 303-972-4894; e-mail: CNFSueLS@aol.com
- National Telemedia Council, Inc., 120 East Wilson Street, Madison, WI 53703; 608-257-7712; e-mail: NTelemedia@aol.com
- New Mexico Media Literacy Project (NMMLP), c/o Albuquerque Academy, 6400 Wyoming NE, Albuquerque, NM 87109; 505-828-3264; e-mail: mccannon@aa.edu; URL: http://www.aa.edu/www.html
- PRIIME TIIME Today, P. O. Box 2829, Littleton, CO 80161; 303-770-3239
- Rocky Mountain Media Watch, Box 18858, Denver, CO 80218; 303-832-7558
- Strategies for Media Literacy, Inc., 1095 Market Street, Suite 410, San Francisco, CA 94103; 415-621-2911; e-mail: medialit@sirius.com

INDEX